Rasbora heteromorpha (*Harlequin Fish*)

A FISHKEEPER'S GUIDE TO
THE TROPICAL AQUARIUM

Poecilia reticulata (*Guppy*)

No. 16061

Barbus conchonius (*Rosy Barb*)

A FISHKEEPER'S GUIDE TO

THE TROPICAL AQUARIUM

A superbly illustrated practical guide to all aspects
of setting up a freshwater tropical aquarium

Dick Mills

Tetra🐾Press

No. 16061

A Salamander Book

Trichogaster leeri (*Pearl Gourami*)

Credits

Editor: Geoff Rogers Designer: Roger Hyde
Colour reproductions:
Chelmer Litho Reproductions
David Bruce Graphics
Rodney Howe Ltd.
Bantam Litho Ltd.
Filmset: SX Composing Ltd.
Printed in Belgium by Henri Proost & Cie, Turnhout.

Author

The author, Dick Mills, has been keeping fishes for over 20 years, during which time he has written many articles for aquatic hobby magazines as well as five books. A member of his local aquarist society, for the past 13 years he has also been a Council member of the Federation of British Aquatic Societies, for which he regularly lectures and produces a quarterly News Bulletin. By profession, he composes electronic music and special sound sequences for television and radio programmes — a complete contrast to fishkeeping, the quietest of hobbies.

Consultant

Fascinated by fishkeeping from early childhood, Dr. Neville Carrington devised an internationally known liquid food for young fishes while studying for a pharmacy degree. After obtaining his Doctorate in Pharmaceutical Engineering Science and a period in industry, Dr. Carrington now pursues his life-long interest in developing equipment and chemical products for the aquarium world.

Contents

A photographic introduction to
more than 50 species suitable
for a first collection.

1 Introduction

A fully stocked freshwater tropical aquarium is immediately exciting visually, and almost demands a closer look into its colourful mysteries. It is at once tranquillizing, which is why many decorative aquariums are situated in public 'stress-making' areas – in hospitals, dentists' waiting rooms, hotel foyers, etc.

In addition, an aquarium involves many other interests, such as biology, geography, physics, chemistry and mathematics. (It must be stressed, however, that these subjects are not obligatory, but are unconsciously and painlessly assimilated and used by any owner of an aquarium.)

Another advantage is that the effort required of the aquarium-keeper is relatively small when compared with other forms of pet-keeping. The animals – in this case, fishes – need no exercising or grooming, and are hardly a restriction on one's normal lifestyle.

Questions often asked by a doubtful would-be fishkeeper are: 'Will I be able to cope with the technicalities?' and 'How do you remember all the scientific names?' Modern fishkeeping has escaped from the rigours and difficulties that pioneering aquarists had to surmount in years gone by; today it is almost enough to say that if you can connect an electrical plug, you can keep tropical fish. The technology is totally reliable and should hold no terrors for anyone. Even youngsters (with a certain amount of adult supervi-

sion) may be encouraged to set up a freshwater tropical tank.

As for the scientific names, there are many thousands of fishkeepers who appreciate the beauty of their fishes and plants without ever knowing their correct taxonomic names – the fishes still swim and the plants still grow, proving once again that ignorance can be bliss!

The main contribution that an aquarist has to make (in addition to the initial financial outlay) is that of understanding how the aquarium works: how the fishes depend upon being given the correct living environment, and how that environment must be maintained. Learning about the actual fishes is a later joy, which may be seen as a reward for the preparatory work done earlier.

The aim of this book is to provide a sound foundation on which your fishkeeping may flourish; once proficiency in keeping the aquarium conditions stable has been achieved, you can then move on to selecting the types of fishes that you wish to keep. A selection of suitable species is included at the end of this guide.

By following the guidance provided in these pages, you will get your fishkeeping off to a good start – but the author will accept no responsibility for the extent to which your life may be taken over by keeping these beautiful fishes. He only hopes that you will find it as fulfilling as he has done. Good fishkeeping!

Tank selection

The size of aquarium you choose not only depends on how much room you have vacant for it (and how much you want to spend on it), but also fixes the size of the fish population you can keep in it.

As the aquarium water is a static body it will be liable to changes in its composition through the presence of the fishes and the action of plants. In order to minimize the effects of these changes a reasonably large body of water is advisable, at least 91 litres (20 gallons). Such a volume of water can be contained in aquariums of many shapes but here again we take heed of the fishes' requirements – something we bear in mind throughout the planning, setting up and maintenance of the aquarium.

The number of fishes that any given volume of water can support depends on the level of dissolved oxygen in the water, how easily it can be replenished, and how easily toxic gases (such as carbon dioxide) can be expelled. These last two processes occur naturally at the water surface, and so a logical arrangement for optimum fish numbers for any given volume of water is one where an adequate depth of water is combined with the largest practicable water surface area. The diagram shows that, although a deep tank might appear to provide ample swimming space, turning the tank on its side retains the same swimming space but gives the added advantage of a much larger surface area.

The 'double-cube' tank (60×30×30cm/24×12×12in) is the usual starting size, although the 38cm

Below: *The two tanks shown here will hold exactly the same amount of water but the one on the right has twice the surface area of the other and will therefore hold twice as many fishes. This is reflected in the drawings of the surface areas shown at the bottom of the page.*

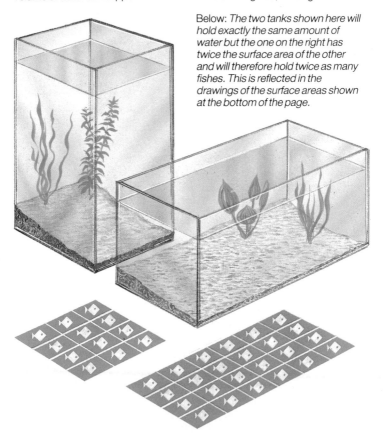

(15in) deep tank is a more pleasing shape. The optimum surface area will provide adequate gaseous exchange, but the theoretical total number of fishes has yet to be calculated. A practicable guide is to allow 75cm^2 (12in^2) for every 2.5cm (1in) of fish body length. For example, an aquarium with a water surface area of 1800cm^2 (288in^2) will comfortably support a total of 60cm (24in) of fish. (A certain amount of common sense needs to be applied, of course; 24 fishes each 2.5cm (1in) long would be quite happy, but two 30cm (12in) fishes or one 60cm (24in) fish certainly wouldn't be!) This calculation is for tropical freshwater fishes only; the needs of coldwater freshwater fishes and tropical marine fishes are quite different. Incidentally, when measuring a fish, the standard length is that measured from the tip of the snout to the end of the body; the tail is excluded.

Types of tank
Modern technology has resulted in today's tanks looking much smarter than the outdated angle-iron framed, putty-glazed models (with their eventual rusting problems). The tanks now commercially available are of two types of construction: small and medium sizes may be made of transparent plastic formed in a single process; and 'all-glass' tanks come in any size and – thanks to the ability to bond glass to glass with silicone rubber adhesives – in many shapes.

Tanks are commercially available in standard lengths or in standard volumes, but if you find difficulty in obtaining a tank of the exact proportions for your requirements, it is possible to make your own tank. The glass used should be optically clear (for the front glass, anyway) and of sufficient thickness to withstand the considerable water pressure exerted on it. Built-in tanks need not be of all-glass construction; glass-fronted wooden, fibre-glass or even concrete tanks are just as serviceable, and there is only one piece of glass to cut and handle.

What has remained unchanged, however, is the weight of a fully set-up aquarium, and for this reason the site has to be chosen with care. The site should be firm, level and smooth; any unevenness in the tank's supporting surface could cause stresses in the glass, with disastrous results. A thick slab of expanded polystyrene placed beneath the tank will safeguard against this danger. A desk top or bureau is not a good place for an aquarium, because the furniture legs may not be strong enough to support it; specially made tank stands are available but remember to protect carpets against damage by their metal legs. If you are building the aquarium into an alcove, make sure the weight is distributed across the floor joists; similarly, aquariums built into walls or unused chimneys need adequate support.

Position of the tank
Some sites are quite unsuitable for an aquarium. A window location receiving direct sunshine each day

Below: *Most tanks are made of glass sheets bonded together with silicone rubber adhesive. Smaller tanks are available in 'seamless' plastic.*

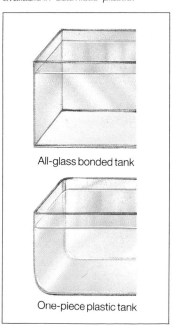

All-glass bonded tank

One-piece plastic tank

TANK SIZES AND CAPACITIES

Tank size	Surface area	Volume	Weight of water	Maximum fish capacity
45×25×25cm (18×10×10in)	1125cm^2 (180in^2)	27 litres (6 gallons)	27kg (60lb)	38cm (15in)
60×30×30cm (24×12×12in)	1800cm^2 (288in^2)	54 litres (12 gallons)	54kg (120lb)	60cm (24in)
60×30×38cm (24×12×15in)	1800cm^2 (288in^2)	68 litres (15 gallons)	68kg (150lb)	60cm (24in)
90×30×38cm (36×12×15in)	2700cm^2 (432in^2)	104 litres (23 gallons)	104kg (230lb)	90cm (36in)
120×30×38cm (48×12×15in)	3600cm^2 (576in^2)	136 litres (30 gallons)	136kg (300lb)	120cm (48in)

Above: *This summary table of common tank sizes and capacities highlights how much full tanks weigh.*

Below: *How fully furnished aquaria can brighten the home – in a corner (left) or as a room divider (right).*

should be avoided: over-heating and excessive green algae growth may occur in summer and possible over-cooling in winter. A position opposite a constantly used door might cause problems, too.

The best place is where total control of the aquarium's temperature and lighting is possible, and where the aquarium will do the most for your decor – in short, a dark unused alcove next to a chimney.

Provision must be made for easy access to the aquarium for maintenance purposes, and there should be convenient power sockets ready for the heating, lighting and other technical requirements of the aquarium.

Installing the tank

A small tank (up to 60cm/24in long) can be partly furnished with rocks and gravel before being placed in position, but larger tanks must be furnished *in situ*. Should you prefer to have a decorative background to your tank, remember to fix this in place first of all!

It is prudent to test any tank for leaks. New ones shouldn't leak, but secondhand tanks (often a good moneysaver) sometimes do. Testing for leaks (especially if you suspect that one exists) is best done outdoors; if a leak is found, the tank should be emptied and dried thoroughly, and the leak sealed with silicone rubber sealant. (Another good reason for checking outdoors is that the sealant gives off strong fumes, and should be used only in a well-ventilated area.) Use a recommended *aquarium* sealant; other sealants, although effective, may contain mildew retardants that can be toxic to fishes. It is advisable to allow the sealant to 'cure' for at least 24 hours before refilling (or re-testing) the tank and using it.

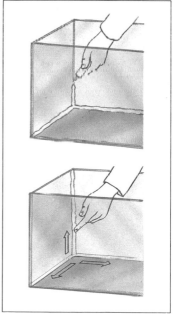

Above: *All-glass fish tanks can be resealed using the recommended silicone rubber adhesive. Apply as shown to interior seams and leave for at least 24 hours before using.*

Heating

In order to keep tropical fishes alive, the temperature of their aquarium water must be maintained at its natural level, i.e. around 24°C (75°F). This is easily accomplished and nothing for the novice fishkeeper to be unduly worried about.

Today's modern aquarium hardware is completely reliable, simple to install and safe to handle. It is not expensive to run, and an average-sized aquarium requires around 250 watts electrical consumption for its full operation. The heating apparatus is thermostatically controlled, and the lighting is not used at night, so the actual consumption is much lower than the estimate.

Aquarists owning many tanks may find it more economical to heat the room space instead of individual tanks; electrical or gas appliances can be used to good effect in this case, both being thermostatically controlled as required. Paraffin oil heaters can also be used, but care must be taken periodically to remove the film of oil that forms on the aquarium water surface with this form of heating.

Heat conservation (and fuel saving, too) can be achieved by insulating the outside of the side and rear walls and the bottom of the tank with expanded polystyrene sheets.

In the event of power failure, temperatures fall quite slowly (or very slowly in large tanks) and should not cause concern unless power failure is prolonged. Should this occur, bottles of hot water (heated by alternative means) can be stood in the tank (beware of overflowing) to restore the temperature to its required value again, or to prevent further heat losses. Covering the aquarium with a blanket will also conserve heat in an emergency.

Temperature is easily measured by means of a simple aquarium thermometer, which may be of a floating or adhesive type. Again, modern technology has provided an up-to-date version in the form of a flat, liquid crystal display.

The majority of aquarium heating is achieved by means of combined heater and thermostat units. Needing

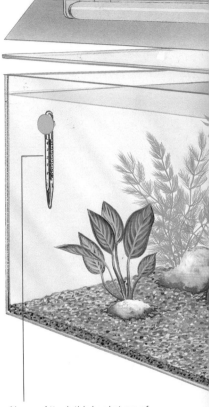

Above: *Attach this basic type of thermometer to the inside glass at a convenient height for easy reading.*

Below: *Fix liquid crystal types (right) on the outside glass; sealed dial versions (left) on the inside glass.*

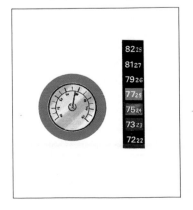

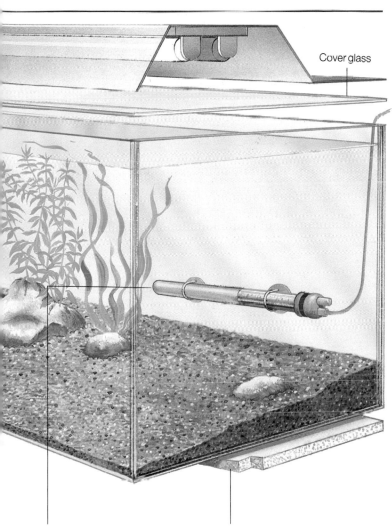

Cover glass

Above: A combined heater-thermostat will prove adequate for most small and medium-sized tanks. Mount it as shown on the rear wall at an angle or nearly vertical in a corner.

Above: A thick piece of expanded polystyrene cut to size and placed underneath the tank will cushion any irregularities in the supporting surface and help to conserve heat.

only the minimum of wiring and taking up less room in the aquarium, these trouble-free units have largely replaced the separate heater and thermostat arrangement favoured by fishkeepers for many years.

The heater/thermostat is housed in a watertight glass tube and is held in position in the aquarium by specially designed retaining clips; these clips,

of non-toxic plastics, are anchored by suction pads to the aquarium glass.

Where separate units are used, the thermostat may be one of two types – internal (submerged type), which looks very similar to a heater, or external (outside the aquarium), which is clipped to the aquarium side and senses the changes in water temperature through the glass.

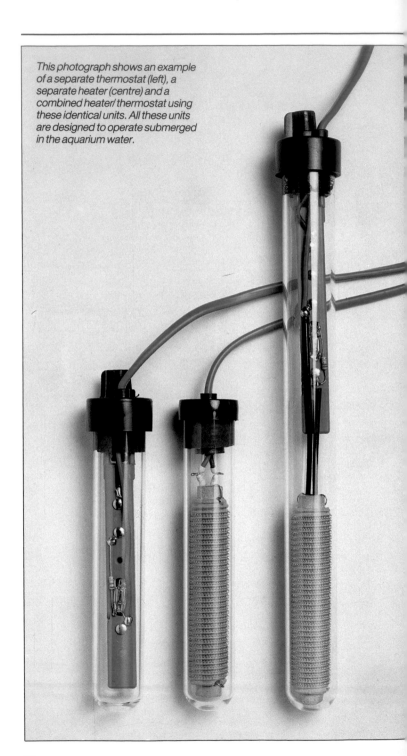

This photograph shows an example of a separate thermostat (left), a separate heater (centre) and a combined heater/thermostat using these identical units. All these units are designed to operate submerged in the aquarium water.

Relatively recent developments have produced designs of thermostats that use microchip circuitry for even more accurate temperature control.

The aquarium heater should be the correct size for the tank. An approximate guide is to allow 10 watts per 4.5 litres (1 gallon) of aquarium capacity. Aquarium heaters are available in 'standard' sizes (50, 75, 100, 125, 150, 200, 300 watts) and the heater that most nearly matches your aquarium's needs should be chosen. In our earlier example, the 60×30×30cm tank (holding 54 litres/12 gallons) would require 120 watts of heating; a 125 watt heater would be ideal. Remember to take into consideration the lowest temperature which the room falls to (central heating systems are usually programmed to go off at night) and the aquarium heater must be able to cope with the extra demand during the winter.

An over-large heater in a small tank could lead to a very rapid rise in temperature if the thermostat got stuck in the 'ON' state. A small heater would be inadequate for a large tank, and could cause thermostat damage.

To provide an even spread of heat throughout large tanks (90cm/36in and upwards) it is normal practice to use two heater/thermostats totalling the required heat wattage.

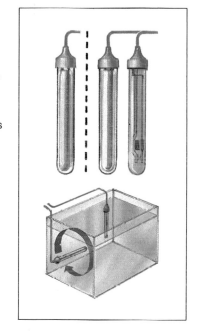

Above: Extra heaters (left of dotted line at top) can be added to an existing heater and thermostat setup to provide additional heat for large tanks. Separate heaters and thermostats should be well spaced in the tank for optimum heat control.
Below: This separate thermostat has a submerged sensor and microchip circuitry for accurate heat control.

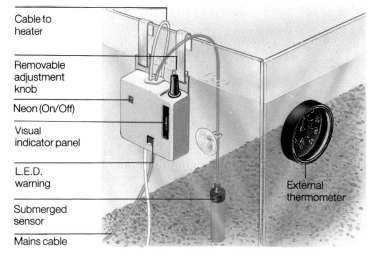

Cable to heater

Removable adjustment knob

Neon (On/Off)

Visual indicator panel

L.E.D. warning

Submerged sensor

Mains cable

External thermometer

Installation

1 To provide the most efficient heating, heaters should be installed in the lowest part of the aquarium water. Normal practice is to position the heater so that it will be hidden by plants or rocks, but there should be free circulation of water around the heater, so mount it clear of the gravel.
2 Combined units may be too long to be mounted vertically in one corner, in which case they can be used diagonally along the rear or side of the tank. Check whether adjusting controls are totally watertight or whether the unit must be installed semi-submerged.
3 Large tanks should have combined heater/thermostats at each end.

4 Make all electrical connections *outside* the tank away from water. A proprietary junction box called a 'cable tidy' will enable all connections to be made safely and neatly. If you are unsure of your electrical wiring ability, always consult a qualified electrician.
5 A heater must always be under water when switched on.
6 Thermostats, generally factory set at around 24°C (75°F), are adjustable a few degrees either way to allow for special temperature requirements.
7 Before making any adjustments to the heating system, or to any other electrical equipment associated with the aquarium, disconnect the equipment from the power supply.

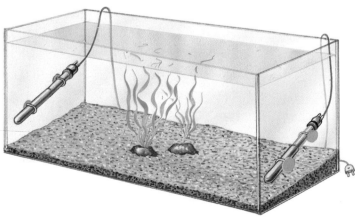

Install the heating equipment in the dry tank after the gravel. Centre left: A common type of combined heater-thermostat being fixed at an angle to the rear wall of the tank. Suitable rubber suckers and clips are provided by the manufacturer. Right: A separate heater controlled by an internal thermostat (top) and an external thermostat (centre); this has a heat sensor on the back of the unit resting against the glass of the aquarium.

Below left: A schematic drawing to show how two heater-thermostat combined units should be arranged to maintain the water temperature in a reasonably large tank. Below right: Another way of heating a large tank using two separate heaters and one external thermostat controlling both of them. Heaters governed by separate thermostats should be well clear of the gravel in the tank to ensure good water circulation around them as they operate.

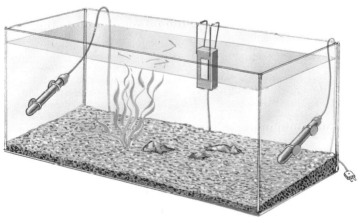

Lighting

Besides making an aquarium look more attractive, light is also an essential stimulus to the plants and fishes. Aquarium plants need light to photosynthesize – a process by which they remove carbon dioxide from the water. In nature, fishes are lit from above by the sun, and any strong side-lighting tends to makes them lean over.

Light can be easily provided by means of lamps mounted in the aquarium cover, usually referred to as the hood or reflector. To simulate the fishes' natural light in brightness and intensity is difficult, given the restrictions imposed by the dimensions of the hood, but luckily the home aquarium appears to be able to function quite happily with much less light. Tungsten lamps, fluorescent tubes, or a combination of the two can be used, each system having both advantages and disadvantages.

Aquatic plants require certain wavelengths of light for optimum growth and special fluorescent lamps are available with these wavelength outputs emphasized. Many aquarists combine several fluorescent tubes of different colours to provide the type of lighting that they find works best, each tube being independently switched.

An approximate guide to the amount of light required is to allow 40 watts (tungsten) or 10 watts (fluorescent) for every 30cm (12in) length of the aquarium, and the aquarium should be lit for at least 10 hours each day. The exact amount and duration of light required is best found by trial and error – enough light to promote good plant growth, but not enough to encourage the unsightly (and often uncontrollable) growth of algae.

Aquariums are often very well furnished with plants – particularly those of Dutch aquarists, who practise 'underwater gardening' so expertly. These aquariums need a much higher intensity of light levels, perhaps four to six times higher than the requirements outlined above.

Cover glasses are necessary to reduce evaporation losses, and to

Above: *This hood incorporates both tungsten and fluorescent lighting. Tungsten lamps are inexpensive and simple to install but they run hot, are 'single coloured' and consume a fair amount of electricity. Fluorescent lamps are expensive to buy and need special starting circuitry but they run cool, can be bought in many 'colours' and produce an even light at low cost.*

stop dust entering the aquarium. They also protect the floating plant leaves from becoming scorched, and the light fittings from condensation damage, and they prevent fishes from leaping out of the aquarium. Cover glasses should be kept spotlessly clean to minimize light losses, and the reflector/hood should be equally well maintained. If tungsten lamps are used, the hood should be well ventilated to reduce a build-up of heat within the hood, which otherwise might shorten lamp life and even raise the temperature of the surface layers of the water to an unacceptable level. Such over-heating can kill fishes.

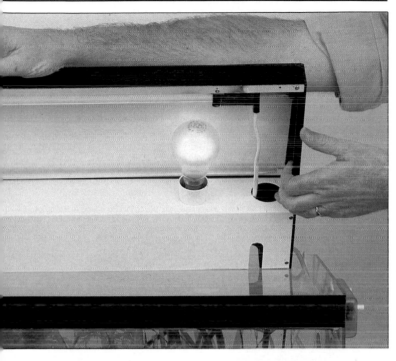

Below: *A centrally placed lamp casts shadows forward; to be avoided.*
Bottom: *A lamp at the front casts shadows away from the viewer; ideal.*

Back   Front

Installation of lighting

Modern aquarium hood/reflectors usually come with ready-made holes for tungsten lamp fittings, and in some more expensive hoods clips are provided for fluorescent tubes together with space for the bulky starter equipment. The use of waterproof connectors in either case is recommended. The aquarium cover glass will prevent water being splashed onto the hot lamps, but be careful (if fluorescent lighting is used) that the extra heavy hood is not dropped onto the cover glass or it may crack it. Fluorescent light starting equipment can be housed remotely from the tank if necessary.

Many hoods are hinged, or have feeding hatches built into them for ease of access at feeding times; a small aperture in the cover glass immediately below the hatch will make feeding even easier. The reflector can be painted white inside or lined with silver foil to give maximum efficiency, and the lamps positioned to give the correct lighting into the aquarium (see diagram).

Aeration

Novice fishkeepers often think it obligatory to have a column of air bubbles constantly rising through the aquarium water, as this condition is to be found in practically all aquatic shops. However, this is not completely necessary and the use of air in the aquarium is sometimes not fully understood.

The benefit of aeration is not quite as obvious as it seems. The belief that oxygen is somehow forced into the water by means of the air bubbles is a misconception. The value of aeration lies more in its ability to create turbulence at the water surface, and to assist circulation of water from the bottom of the tank to the top (something that the processes of heating and filtration and the movements of the fish also do to some extent).

Turbulence on the surface of the water effectively increases the water surface area, which, as we have already learnt, plays an important role in the replenishment of oxygen in the water and the removal of carbon dioxide from it. This, in turn, allows more fishes to be kept in the tank than theoretical calculations suggest (see page 13). However, the use of aeration should not be taken as an excuse for crowding more fishes into the tank.

for if the air supply fails for any length of time, the tank will become over-crowded, although the risk to the fishes is from possible asphyxiation rather than from sheer numbers of fishes together.

A supply of air is provided by an air pump, which is electrically powered; there are two types of air pump – vibrator and piston type. The most popular type of air pump is the simple vibrator design, which is available in many sizes. It is reasonably quiet in operation and needs little maintenance. Piston air pumps can be more expensive but some fishkeepers prefer their obvious 'mechanical' appearance. They require more maintenance but usually make less noise than the cheaper vibrator models.

Pumped air is fed to the aquarium by means of plastic tubing. The flow of air may be regulated either with clamps or with air valves. Some higher-priced air pumps have an air control fitted; this may be an air-bleed screw, or a potentiometer (or variable resistance) in the pumps voltage supply. The air is broken up into a column of bubbles by passing it through a submerged airstone, usually a block of porous ceramic material or hardwood.

Below: *The vibrator air pump (right) is inexpensive and robust. The piston type (left) has a 'mechanical fascination' for many fishkeepers.*

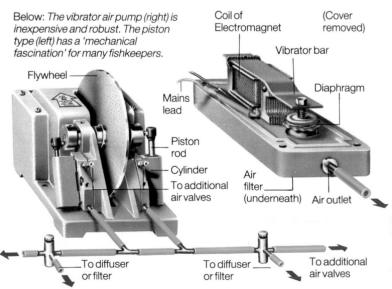

Coil of Electromagnet

(Cover removed)

Vibrator bar

Flywheel

Mains lead

Diaphragm

Piston rod

Cylinder

To additional air valves

Air filter (underneath)

Air outlet

To diffuser or filter

To diffuser or filter

To additional air valves

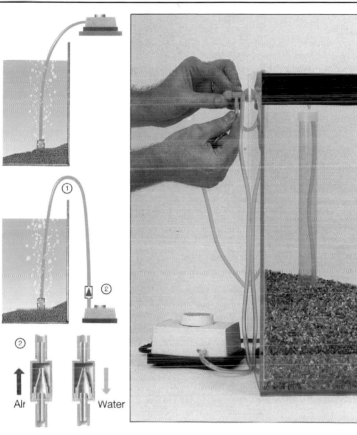

Above: *How to stop water siphoning
back into the air pump by (top)
placing the pump above water level or
(centre) making an 'anti-siphon' loop
(1) at least 5cm(2in) high. The lower
diagrams show that a one-way check
valve (2) allows air through (left) but
closes against water pressure (right).
The photograph shows an airline
connected to a ganged valve.*

Air   Water

Installing the air system

The pump should be placed, ideally,
above the water level of the aquarium,
to prevent water siphoning into the
pump if the electrical supply fails.
Alternatively, as most hobbyists seem
to site their air pumps on a handy
shelf below the aquarium, an 'anti-
siphon loop' is made in the airline,
looping it a few centimetres above the
water level to prevent back-
siphoning. A commercially available
'one-way' check valve also prevents
back-siphoning. If extra equipment is
to be fed from the one air supply, the
air is first fed into a multi-way ganged
valve, which allows independent
control of the air supplies; a spare
position on this multi-way valve can
also be used to bleed off excessive air
from the system.

Some inexpensive vibrator pumps
will have an annoying buzz to them.
Enclosing them in a cupboard will
deaden the noise somewhat, but a
close-fitting, foam-filled box is better;
ventilation holes should be left to
prevent the air pump from over-
heating and to allow a free passage of
air. Most pumps have a felt-pad air
filter mounted underneath – keep it
clean! Piston pumps require regular
oiling, and an oil-trap should be fitted
in the airline to prevent oil reaching the
aquarium and affecting the fishes.

Filtration

So far, sufficient space, oxygen, heat and light have been provided for the fishes in correct quantities, and we have arranged for these conditions to be held as stable as possible. However, the presence of living animals and plants in the aquarium will upset the stable environment we have created unless further steps are taken to prevent deterioration of the water's wholesomeness.

The living aquarium produces waste products from several sources. The fishes excrete liquid and solid matter which produces ammonia; plant leaves die and decompose; uneaten food also rots. The water takes on a slightly amber coloration and may even begin to smell. The action of the fishes often causes the water to be less than crystal clear.

Water in a natural environment is subject to change by the effects of wind, rain and – most important of all – a continuous water flow in streams and rivers. Without actually recreating a river course in our aquarium, we can attempt to purify the water (or at least minimize any pollution of it) by two simple means – partial water changes, and filtration.

Partial water changes are self-explanatory: every two or three weeks some 10-20% of the aquarium water is removed and replaced with fresh, ideally at the same temperature, although most fishes appear to enjoy the addition of slightly cooler water, as long as it does not lower the water temperature too drastically. The action will obviously remove some waste material (including dirt from the aquarium floor, if a siphon tube is used to good advantage), and the addition of clean water will dilute the waste products still remaining in the tank. Automatic water changers make this chore less tiresome.

Filtration equipment for the aquarium works in three simple ways: mechanical, chemical or biological. The majority of container-type filters (whether of internal or external design, or of air or electrical operation) are of the first two categories, using some form of medium to trap suspended material in the water flowing through it, and

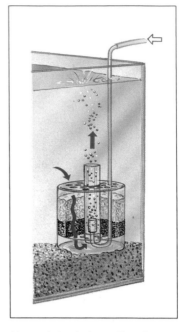

Above: *A simple, internal box filter operated by a pumped air supply.*

some other materials (such as activated carbon, peat, resins) to remove dissolved waste products or to alter the water's properties. Biological filtration is completely different in concept, relying on bacterial action to break down ammonia and nitrites into the less toxic nitrates.

Container-type filters
The general principle of these filters is to pass dirty aquarium water through a medium-filled container (where the dirt is removed) and return the cleaned water to the aquarium. The usual medium is some form of man-made fibre: dacron floss, nylon floss, etc. (Glass wool is not recommended, as tiny fragments of glass can be transferred into the aquarium with the risk of injuries to the fishes.) Some modern filters have tailor-made filter pads of foam material, but do not attempt to do it yourself with, say, polyurethane foam, because such material may be toxic to fishes.

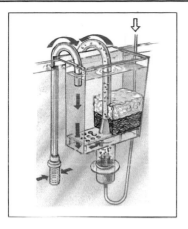

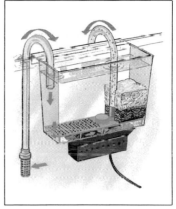

Above: *An external, open-box filter operated by a pumped air supply.*

Above: *The same basic filter as at left but with an electric impeller.*

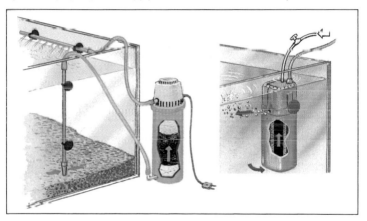

Above: *An external, electrically driven power filter with spray bar.*

Above: *An electric, submerged power filter with aeration control.*

Filters containing activated carbon should not be used if any medication is to be added to the aquarium, because the medication will be adsorbed by the carbon. Aeration should be substituted, as some medicaments reduce the oxygen content of the water.

For a decorative or fully planted aquarium, an outside filtration system is best so that regular maintenance of the filter does not cause disruption to the planted tank.

The external, open-box filter *cannot* overflow (often a worry to beginners). The siphon system into the box from the aquarium automatically stops when the filter box is full, and only when cleaned water is being returned to the aquarium does it start again.

'Power filters' – i.e. electrically powered 'open-box' or 'canister' types – may be used inside or outside the aquarium, and they have a far larger water flow rate. Check all tube connections thoroughly before operating, as a loose pipe can result in an empty tank and a flood elsewhere! This is particularly important where a canister filter is used remote from the aquarium.

Biological filtration

Using nature's own way of dealing with waste products, the biological filter makes use of the aquarium's gravel as a filter bed. The aquarium water is passed through the gravel and a colony of bacteria develops throughout the entire gravel bed. The virtue of this type of filtration is that the hardware is sited invisibly beneath the gravel and needs hardly any maintenance. The natural sequence of events is that waste products from the fish are first converted to toxic *ammonia*. This ammonia is converted to *nitrite* by Nitrosomonas bacteria, then Nitrobacter bacteria turn nitrite into *nitrate*, which is less harmful to fishes and which many plants use as a food material.

A biological filter (usually referred to by hobbyists as an undergravel filter) is generally operated by air from the air pump, although where an extra large water flow is required an electrical water pump can be fitted. If biological filtration is to be used in an aquarium containing fishes that dig or forage a lot in the gravel, then the undergravel filter plate must be protected and not allowed to become exposed. This can be done by putting a piece of nylon netting over the gravel bed one or two centimetres above the filter before the final layers of gravel are put in place.

The biological filtration process depends, as we have seen, on

The airstone provides a stream of bubbles.

The biological filter plate should cover the base of the aquarium to provide the greatest area for the bacterial colony in the gravel.

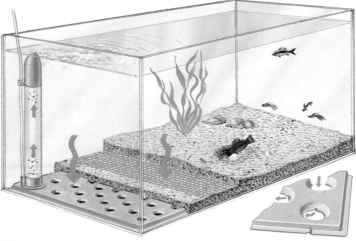

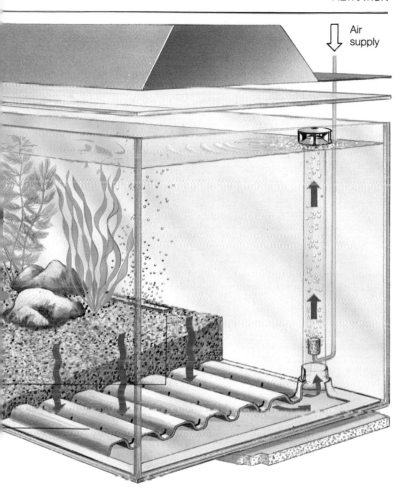

bacterial action, and the bacteria colony is sustained by the flow of oxygenated water through the gravel. For this reason, an undergravel filter should never be switched off, for as soon as the water flow stops, the bacteria colony will begin to die and the action of the filter will be lost.

Left: *A layer of nylon netting fitted one or two centimetres above the filter plate will prevent it being exposed by digging fishes. The detail shows how water flows through the base of the filter plate beneath the gravel.*

Right: *This non-submersible electric water pump is mounted on the top of the biological filter's lift tube.*

29

Installation of filters

Filters are best installed before the addition of various aquarium furnishings, such as rocks and plants, restricts working space.

Provision must be made for easy access to inside filters for maintenance purposes. Unless they are fitted with anchoring suction pads, inside air-operated filters have a tendency to float up, but a few pebbles in the bottom avoid this. A plastic bag slipped under the filter box before removing it from the tank for cleaning will also prevent dirty water spilling back into the tank.

Installation of outside box filters often means that the tank hood has to be modified to accommodate the siphon and return tubes. In large tanks, arrange them so that the returned clean water enters the tank well away (preferably at the other end of the tank) from the filter's intake siphon; this will provide a flow of water across the whole tank.

Where activated carbon is used in a filter system, it should not be the last material that the water passes through before returning to the tank. Activated carbon is often sandwiched between layers of filter floss – the first layer removes suspended dirt from the water, the second prevents particles of carbon being drawn into the aquarium. Alternatively, the carbon can be contained in a cloth bag if used in a filter alone.

Above: *Fit the biological filter first.*
Left: *Cover the plate with a layer of gravel at least 5cm(2in) deep.*
Below: *Slope the gravel from back to front and contour as you wish.*

Above: *Examples of air-operated filters. The simple sponge filter (top) and the internal box filter (shown below it) are both ideal for using in fry-raising, unplanted tanks.*

Left: *External open-box filters that are more suitable for furnished tanks, where their regular maintenance will cause little disturbance to the fishes and the plant arrangements inside the tank. Both of these models are operated by pumped air.*

31

These photographs show a selection of power filters – electrically operated units that provide an increased water flow compared to the air-operated types.

Above: *This model is basically an external box filter with an electric water pump to accelerate the water flow. The filter medium for this model is supplied as an easily replaceable cartridge.*

Above right: *An internal canister-type power filter. Water is drawn up into the base of the canister, passes through the filter medium and is pumped out through the hole near the top of the casing. An airline running into the filter aerates the outgoing water stream as an added bonus.*

Right: *A powerful external canister-type filter. Water is drawn from the just above the gravel bed and, once cleaned, returns to the aquarium through a horizontal spray bar that runs the length of the tank.*

To prevent back-siphoning of water to the air pump, all air-operated filters' air supplies should have an anti-siphon loop in them similar to that suggested for airstones (see Aeration, page 25).

Some electrically driven power filters allow air into the returning water, but care should be taken not to let in too much air, in case the motor-impeller runs 'dry', resulting in rapid wear. The makers' instructions usually make this point quite clear.

In addition to having optional aeration facilities, the sophisticated power filters also allow water flow to be adjusted and for the motor to be cooled by the aquarium water (which also means a saving on the heating bill, as the motor's warmth heats the aquarium water all the time the filter is operating). Other designs permit the easy addition of extra filter modules as required; some filters can even be cleaned and the filter medium replaced without switching off or removing from the tank.

Because of the increased water flow capability of this type of filter, the returning water is usually distributed through a spray bar.

Whatever filter material is used, it should not be packed so tightly into the filter body that the flow of water is impeded. Usually a poor water flow back from a filter indicates that it needs cleaning! (Filter floss can be used again after washing out, so it is in your own interest not to let it get too dirty in the first place.)

Gravel and rocks

Aquarium gravel serves several functions in addition to simply being what one expects to find on the aquarium floor. We have just seen how it provides a home for denitrifying bacteria when used in conjunction with a biological filter; it also serves as a growing medium for rooted aquarium plants, is used as a spawning site by several species of fishes, and acts as a home and night accommodation for some marine fishes; but basically it acts as a background over which the fishes swim.

The latter function of gravel raises the question of what colour is most suitable for the aquarium. When seen from above (the normal viewpoint of a fish predator), fishes' top surface is generally a dark colour, which helps to disguise them as they swim over the river bed. Very few fishes come from areas where the river bed is light-coloured, and fishkeepers have found that using a light-coloured gravel in the aquarium tends to 'wash out' the fishes' colours. The gravel normally available from a dealer is a dark mottled brown/yellow colour, and this suits the purpose very well. Even when used with dissimilar coloured rocks the gravel's colour need not jar, as small particles of rock can be spread over its surface to tone down the discrepancy, so that the gravel appears as in nature, where the water current has brought down fine gravel along the stream's rocky bed.

Brightly coloured gravel is available at aquatic stores but, in addition to the questionable decorative value, there is also the possibility that dyes used to produce these unnatural shades may leak out into the aquarium water and release poisonous substances.

The particle size of the gravel is important. If it is too coarse, food can fall beyond the reach of the fishes and begin to pollute the aquarium water; if it is too fine, plants will have difficulty in rooting, and the water flow through the biological filter will be impeded. A particle size of approximately 2-3mm (0.08-0.1in) is about correct.

Gravel collected by offshore dredging often contains calcium-rich

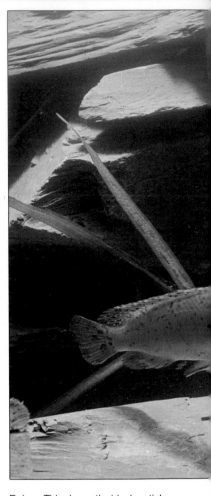

Below: *This shows the ideal particle size for aquarium gravel. Make sure that it is clean before using it.*

sea-shell fragments, which will adversely affect the aquarium water. Many aquatic stores stock lime-free gravel, which is preferable.

The amount of gravel required may surprise you; allow at least a 9 litre (2 gallon) bucketful for every 900cm^2 (1ft^2) of aquarium floor area. If the tank is deep and the gravel is to be landscaped, even more will be required for the final effect.

An aquarium with gravel and plants often looks better after the addition of rocks; and indeed, many fishes come from areas where plants are the exception rather than the rule. As with gravel, the choice of rocks is also governed by colour, size and

Above: *A tank furnished with inert, forbidding looking rocks suits these hard-water Malawi Blue Cichlids.*

composition. Soft, crumbly rocks likely to disintegrate in water are not suitable, neither are jagged rocks, limestones or those bearing obvious mineral ores; an exception can be made for calcareous rocks when these are used in an aquarium containing Rift Valley Cichlids, whose natural habitat is hard water. Granite, basalt, quartz and slate are all safe for aquarium use. Aquarium decorations such as sunken brick walls and terraces (often fashioned in moulded concrete) are not recommended.

Installing gravel and rocks

Gravel must be washed before use. A half-filled bucket of gravel can be conveniently washed at a time under a running hose (until the overflowing water remains clear).

Remember that if you are using biological filtration the filter goes into the tank *before* the gravel.
Large rocks should be sunk well into the gravel (preferably standing on the tank base to prevent toppling).

When building up strata of rocks with slate, avoid using very sharp-edged pieces. Caves and outcrops of rock can be made by glueing pieces of rock together with silicone sealant before placing them in the tank. A backdrop of rocks can be made by glueing rocks directly to the back (and sides) of the aquarium when empty.

Gravel should be banked up towards the rear of the tank; this slope can be maintained by placing pieces of rock into the gravel to act as terrace-like supports.

Rocks can be used to hide heaters and thermostats, but don't overcrowd the aquarium with rocks – remember to leave the fishes some clear swimming space.

Other tank decorations

A most effective decoration is a piece of sunken wood or tree branch. If collected from the wild, any such wood used should be long dead, and waterlogged if possible, with no trace of decay. It should be boiled in several changes of water and be immersed in water for several weeks before aquarium use. There should be no discoloration of the water from tannins in the wood. Dead wood can also be sealed with polyurethane varnish (several coats) before use. Petrified wood can often be obtained from aquatic stores and florists, and makes a good aquarium decoration.

Cork bark is another favourite decoration and is often used as a tank background, or to form terracing. The colour is most pleasing, and bark is easy to cut and shape to the required dimensions.

Synthetic imitation rocks, logs and plants are gaining popularity. These soon lose their artificiality in the

aquarium as they are covered with a film of living algae. Imitation plants will not serve the same purpose as living ones but can be used to good effect to provide greenery in a tank containing very boisterous fishes or those with strong vegetarian habits.

Any tendency for wooden logs to float can be counteracted by fixing a piece of slate to the underside and burying it in the gravel. Similarly a 'log' of cork bark can be induced to lie down by wrapping it around a plastic pipe or bottle filled with gravel, and securing with nylon thread. Most obstinate decorations can be persuaded to stay in place by similar means or by using recommended aquarium silicone adhesives.

The sequence of photographs starting at top left shows how an interesting aquascape can be built up, starting with flat rocks being embedded in a gravel bank, followed by careful positioning of synthetic logs. The final result is shown above.

Below: *Examples of some suitable materials with which to furnish the aquarium. Natural wood should be thoroughly boiled before use.*

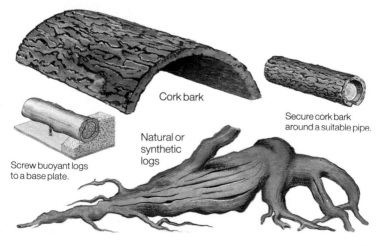

Cork bark

Secure cork bark around a suitable pipe.

Natural or synthetic logs

Screw buoyant logs to a base plate.

37

Water

One of the attractions of keeping tropical freshwater fishes is the wide range of species available. Hardly any body of water anywhere in the world has escaped the collector's net, and supplies of fish are never more than a few hours away, thanks to modern air transport.

It follows that fishes come from many differing locations – streams, rivers, lakes, estuaries – and each location will have a different quality of water, in addition to whether it is flowing or static.

It says much for the hardiness and physical tolerance of aquarium fishes that, despite their various origins, most of them survive very well in the water we provide for them, usually from our domestic supply. To appreciate the fishes' problems, and to understand their requirements more fully so that we can provide suitable living conditions for them, we should take a little time to study water itself – the fishes' own 'atmosphere'.

The water cycle is the most important natural phenomenon on earth, regulating our weather and the growth of food crops. It has no starting or ending point but is a continuous process. For the purposes of our study, we can conveniently join the process at the sea, which covers nearly three quarters of the earth's surface. Water evaporating from the sea condenses into clouds, which deposit pure fresh water as rain over the land masses. This water then finds its way by rivers and underground percolation back to the sea, where the natural cycle begins again.

That is the bare bones of the story of water, but other conditions alter the purity of the water on its long journey back to the sea; as this journey will encompass the living areas of our freshwater fishes we shall follow it in a little more detail.

As rain water falls through the atmosphere it absorbs various salts and gases, and by the time it reaches ground level it is already fairly contaminated, generally being acidic in make-up. Its chemistry is further modified by the nature of the terrain on which the rain falls and over which

Above: *The lakes of the Great Rift Valley in East Africa contain hard, alkaline water that supports unique populations of Cichlid fishes.*
Right: *A simplified representation of the natural water cycle. The rocks, terrain and vegetation all affect the final quality of fresh water.*

the ground water subsequently flows. Water running across granite mountains will be quite different in composition from that seeping through chalk hills; water held in lakes in rocky basins will be different from that in rain-forest streams and rivers.

Sun

Clouds

EVAPORATION

Rain

Sea

Ground water

What is meant by 'different', and can it be measured? There are two types of differences, although they are often interrelated and often confused. They are *pH* and *hardness*.

The pH of water

The pH is simply a scale of values on which the relative acidity or alkalinity may be measured. The numbers on the pH scale (0-14) are logarithmic, so that an increase or decrease of pH 1 is in fact an increase or decrease of the power of 10. The pH 0 is the strongest acid and pH 14 is the strongest alkali.

The middle position, pH 7, is known as the neutral point, being neither acidic nor alkaline.

Fortunately, the range with which we are concerned is a relatively narrow one, between pH 6.6 and 7.5 for normal fishkeeping purposes. In nature, fishes can be found under more extreme conditions – from pH 5.5 (very acid, jungle streams with lots of decaying vegetation) to pH 9 (soda lakes in Africa's Rift Valley).

Water's pH is measured very easily with suitable test kits; these range from simple sensitized papers to elaborate electronic devices, and of course the accuracy is proportional to the cost! The middle-range liquid colour indicators are adequate for hobby purposes, and foolproof.

The manipulation of the water's pH, should it be thought necessary, is a complicated process involving knowledge of water chemistry to a degree impossible to explain here; it includes strict control of everything that may be put into the aquarium water, which may otherwise adversely affect the conditions so carefully created. This area of aquarium technology becomes more significant when attempting to breed those aquarium fishes generally considered to be 'difficult', which demand more attention to detail than the normal community collection.

There is a general relationship between the pH of water and its hardness. Acidic (lower than pH 7) water is usually soft, and alkaline (higher than pH 7) water is hard due to the amount of dissolved minerals.

The stability of pH in the aquarium is not constant and may vary from day to night as the plants' photosynthesis has effect. The water may be more acidic after periods of darkness, so it is a good practice to make any test of the water at the same time of day, and at the same water temperature. The differences in pH due to the natural activity of the aquarium's daily life will not be in excess of, say, 0.1 of a reading, but drastic changes of pH should be investigated – or, to put it the other way round, drastic alterations in fish behaviour or health may be due to changes in the pH.

Below left: *This jungle stream in Sri Lanka is strongly acidic (pH below 7) because of the decaying vegetation that builds up in the water.*

Below: *This pH test kit uses liquid reagents to cause a colour change in the water sample, which is then compared to a colour reference wheel to give a direct pH reading.*

Above: *Dissolved minerals, notably calcium and magnesium salts, make the water in Africa's Rift Valley lakes alkaline in nature (pH above 7).*

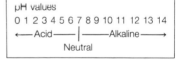

pH values
0 1 2 3 4 5 6 7 8 9 10 11 12 13 14
←——— Acid ——— | ——— Alkaline ——→
Neutral

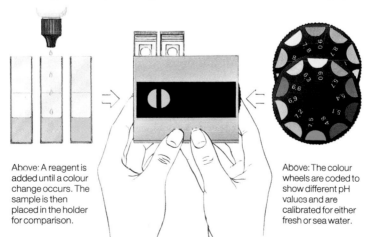

Above: A reagent is added until a colour change occurs. The sample is then placed in the holder for comparison.

Above: The colour wheels are coded to show different pH values and are calibrated for either fresh or sea water.

41

Hardness

Thanks to washing powder and detergent advertising, people are more conversant with water's other characteristic, hardness. Due to dissolved salts (usually of calcium and magnesium) hardness is of two types: temporary, and permanent. The temporary hardness may be removed by boiling, when the soluble calcium bicarbonate is deposited as calcium carbonate, the 'scale' in kettles. Permanent hardness can be removed only by chemical means, by ion exchange, or by distillation. Hardness as a whole can be reduced by dilution, using any known softer water in correct proportions to arrive at the required hardness figure. The calculations are simple: diluting 5 litres of hard water (12 degrees of hardness) with 5 litres of soft water, such as unpolluted rain water (0 degrees), will give 10 litres of water of 6 degrees of hardness.

Hardness can be added to any soft water by including pieces of chalk or limestone in the aquarium decoration, and (as we have already seen) the composition of the aquarium gravel may also harden the water (see Gravel, page 34).

Test kits are available for assessing water hardness; as with determining pH, a simple colour change process occurring in the sample of water to be tested gives an accurate figure.

A slight confusion may arise, because there are several different ways of measuring hardness, and

Above: *The Discus Fish needs soft, bacteria-free water to thrive.*

figures quoted in aquatic books may be from any system. The German fishkeeper measures general (or total) hardness in °GH, and carbonate hardness in °DH. (Hardness due to non-carbonates is calculated by subracting °DH from °GH). English fishkeepers measure hardness by parts per million of calcium carbonate in water, and the figure is known as °Clarke. To add to the confusion, the German °DH is calculated on the amount of calcium oxide (in milligrams) in one litre of water.

Hardness can sometimes be reduced by using peat moss in the aquarium filter. Garden peat, to which chemicals may have been added, should not be used; natural sphagnum moss is recommended. Using peat will also tend to acidify the water (lower the pH) and such measures are often used by fishkeepers specializing in Egg-laying Toothcarps (see page 76).

Below: Labeotropheus trewavasae, *which lives in hard water in Africa.*

Nitrites

Biological filtration effectively reduces the ammonia and nitrogen levels in the water (see Filtration, page 28), and the efficiency of the filter and the 'safeness' of the water can be measured with a Nitrite Test Kit. Freshwater fishes can tolerate a much higher level of nitrites than their marine counterparts, and testing for nitrite levels is usually undertaken more regularly by marine fishkeepers.

The lowering of the nitrite reading over the aquarium's settling-in period is an indication of the maturing of the bacterial colony in the biological filter. The figure reaches a maximum within a few days of the aquarium starting up, and then declines over perhaps the next three weeks to a steady minimum level.

Ammonia, nitrites and nitrates are all part of the nitrogen cycle within the aquarium, and are reduced to non-toxic levels by the biological filter. Very small amounts of ammonia and nitrites can be very poisonous to fishes; and although some fishes may be tolerant to certain levels of nitrite, their immunity or resistance to disease or stress may be seriously impaired as a result.

Salinity

Fishes from brackish water areas such as estuaries, which receive some saltwater from the sea, may thrive better in aquarium water to which some natural sea-salt has been added. This is usually given at the rate

Above: *This Fingerfish,* Monodactylus argenteus, *lives naturally in fresh, brackish and sea water. Add some sea salt crystals to the tank water.*

of 2-3 teaspoonsful per 9 litres (2 gallons) of aquarium water. Many live-bearers, particularly Mollies, also benefit from the addition of salt but the dosage should be halved.

During water changes replacement water may be similarly treated, but evaporation losses should be made good only with *fresh* water. The growth of some plants may be affected by the addition of salt to the water. Some Catfishes may be intolerant of brackish water also.

Water additives

Many patent additives are said to assist the fishkeeper in making the domestic supply water more suitable for fish life. These include dechlorinators, heavy metal precipitators, and water tonics said to help simulate certain natural water conditions as found in the fishes' original home. If these are added, together with other additives such as plant foods and maybe health cures, the aquarist will have a difficult time assessing just what is the final composition of the aquarium water. It may be prudent to exercise some restraint on what is added to the aquarium. Medicaments are best used in a separate aquarium, where the dosage can be more accurately measured and results monitored.

Use of domestic supply water

Although water from the tap is primarily produced for human consumption, it is normally quite suitable for aquarium use provided one or two precautions are taken. Water that has been standing in copper pipes (particularly newly installed pipework) may be toxic to fishes, so let the tap run for a few minutes before using any water from it. Heavily chlorinated water should be strongly aerated to disperse the chlorine before the fishes are introduced. Some aquarists add dechlorinating additives, and the manufacturer's instructions should be closely followed for these.

The apparent problem of our fishes' needs for different water conditions can be put into perspective by realizing that many of our fishes do not come from where we think they do! Many are aquarium bred in commercial quantities, thousands of miles from their native homes. Added to this, the fishes at your local aquatic store will have been

Below: *Two different ways to fill the tank without disturbing the gravel.*
Below right: *The tank ready to receive plants; incomplete filling prevents overflowing when planting.*

kept in similar water conditions to yours, before you buy them. A responsible dealer will give you all the information you need on the water conditions needed for his stock if this is different from the local supply.

Filling the aquarium

The aquarium, with gravel, rocks and any other tank decorations in place, and fitted with UNCONNECTED heating and filtration equipment, is now ready to be filled with water.

To prevent the water from destroying the contours of the gravel and washing away rock formations, take care when filling. A small jug or saucer standing on the aquarium gravel can break the force of the jet of water out of the hosepipe; the overflow will gently fill the aquarium.

Fill the tank to half way with cold water, then add warm water to bring the level up to three quarters full for planting. Water with the chill taken off will not shock the plants (or your hands) too much.

After planting, fill the tank with more warm water so that no waterline is showing below the tank frame or decorative trim. Any film of dirt on the water surface can be removed by drawing a lightweight sheet of paper slowly across the surface.

TANK CAPACITIES AND RECOMMENDED HEATER SIZES			
Tank size	Volume	Weight of water	Recommended heater size
45×25×25cm (18×10×10in)	27 litres (6 gallons)	27kg (60lb)	75w
60×30×30cm (24×12×12in)	54 litres (12 gallons)	54kg (120lb)	125w
60×30×38cm (24×12×15in)	68 litres (15 gallons)	68kg (150lb)	150w
90×30×38cm (36×12×15in)	104 litres (23 gallons)	104kg (230lb)	2×125w
120×30×38cm (48×12×15in)	136 litres (30 gallons)	136kg (300lb)	2×150w

Aquarium plants

Aquarium plants are available in many forms and contrasting shades. They look nice, and we have already discussed the important role they play in keeping the aquarium healthy; and plants also provide shade, refuge, spawning sites and (in some cases) food for the fishes.

The choice of plants is almost as wide as that of fishes. Plants can be selected to occupy different areas of the tank, from floating plants on the water surface to aquarium floor-covering miniature grasses. Leaf forms may be strap-like, feathery, or broad. Colours range from light to dark green, and some leaves have reddish purple undersides. Flowers in the aquarium are not rare either, and you can obtain seeds from certain species of plants, from which to grow fresh stock.

Most aquatic plants conform to the conventional idea of plants: a root system, above which grows the stalk and leaves. However, not all aquarium plants are rooted in the gravel, and many of those that are can also obtain nourishment directly from the water through their leaves. Some species cling to the surface of roots and submerged logs, but others have no fixed location, freely floating on the water surface, their trailing hair-like roots providing a sanctuary for tiny fishes.

Being totally submerged, the majority of aquatic plants reproduce by sending out runners or developing daughter plants on existing leaves. Many of the bushy, feathery-leaved plants can be multiplied by means of cuttings, where a top portion of the plant is removed and re-rooted in the

Right: *The diagonal arrangement of these plants of various colour and shape creates a sense of perspective.*

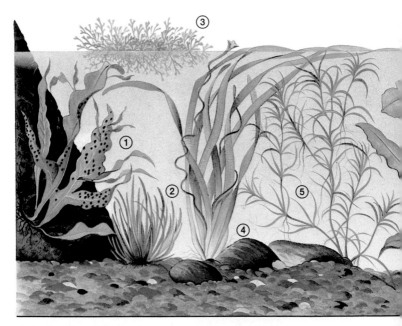

1 Microsorium pteropus
The rootstock clings to logs and rocks. Thrives in any light conditions.
2 Acorus gramineus var pusillus
Grows slowly in the aquarium. Prefers cool water conditions. A good choice as a foreground plant in the aquarium.

3 Riccia fluitans
Ideal for shading the aquarium and as a fry refuge. Some fish eat it.
4 Vallisneria natans
Excellent as a background plant.
5 Najas guadalupensis
Dense clumps ideal for spawning.

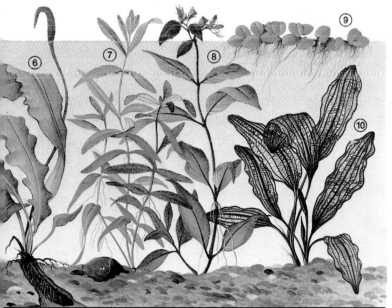

6 Aponogeton crispus
Grows from a rhizome. Will flower above the surface. Cool rest in winter.
7 Hygrophila polysperma
Fast growing. Easily propagated.
8 Nomaphila stricta
For hard water. May be eaten by snails.

9 Salvinia natans
Trailing roots provide excellent shelter for fry. Spreads quickly on surface.
10 Aponogeton madagascariensis
Needs bright light, water changes and a rest period to grow well.

gravel to grow as a new independent plant. Some species will develop roots from a single severed leaf, which will also provide a new plant.

When planting the aquarium, try to disguise the boxiness of the tank; careful planting can create an illusion of continuing space within the four walls of the aquarium. However, creating space is not done by planting regimented avenues of single plants in the manner of orchard trees. Plants should be grown in species clumps as they would occur in nature.

The mature aquarium should be capable of sustaining plant growth with nutrients generated within itself. A newly set-up tank can be given encouragement by providing additional liquid plant-food, by planting the plants in special nutrient-rich preformed plugs, or by adding peat, loam or clay to the aquarium gravel. Any such additions should be treated with caution, particularly by the newcomer, as early experiments in underwater horticulture do not always bring the hoped-for success.

The shape of a plant dictates its use in the aquarium. Tall, grassy plants such as *Vallisneria* and *Sagittaria* are ideal for the back and sides of the tank; even if the leaves grow taller than the water depth, their progress across the surface of the water brings shade to the fishes.

Bushy plants can be used to fill in corners and gaps between rocky outcrops. Cuttings taken from such plants encourage the original plant to develop more side-shoots. Typical species include water wisteria (*Synnema triflorum,* also known as *Hygrophila difformis*), *Hygrophila polysperma, Nomaphila stricta, Cabomba caroliniana, Ceratophyllum demersum, Ludwigia repens* and *Ceratopteris thalictroides.*

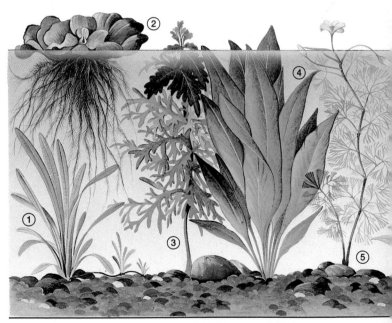

1 Sagittaria subulata
Popular plant; similar to Vallisneria.
2 Pistia stratiotes
The roots give shelter for young fish.
3 Hygrophila difformis
Leaves vary in shape depending on the strength of lighting. Roots easily.

4 Echinodorus bleheri
Very popular as a specimen plant. Plantlets form on long runners.
5 Cabomba caroliniana
Widely grown. An excellent spawning medium. Needs clean water to keep leaves sediment free. Roots easily.

Above: The fishes and plants in this aquarium have been carefully chosen to contrast and complement each other. Note how the red of the fishes at top centre reflects the colour of the plants at bottom left. The silvery shapes of the other fishes add sharp brilliance and movement to the scene.

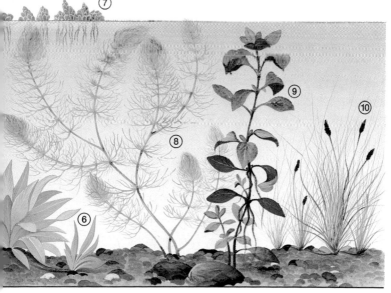

6 Echinodorus magdalenensis
An ideal foreground plant. Sends out many runners bearing young plants.
7 Azolla caroliniana
Floating plant with velvety leaves, often red-tinged. Provides a shady haven for young fishes. Shown raised.

8 Ceratophyllum demersum
Shown rooted but usually grows in a floating tangle. Grow from cuttings.
9 Ludwigia repens
A superb plant for bright aquariums.
10 Eleocharis acicularis
Interesting form; needs good light.

The floor of the aquarium can benefit from generous plantings of miniature species of *Cryptocoryne*, and larger varieties look well in front of rocks. There is no need to worry about these bottom-hugging plants being starved of light by their loftier neighbours, as they are quite used to lower light levels.

For spectacular specimen plants – often rivalling the fish for popularity – members of the *Echinodorus* and *Aponogeton* families are hard to beat. Such plants may be rooted in miniature flowerpots sunk in the gravel, where they can be pampered if necessary, as befits the 'stars' of the plant population.

Azolla, *Riccia* and *Salvinia* are all floating species of minute proportions, whereas *Pistia* is very large, often finding the cramped space beneath the hood rather limiting to its ambitious growth.

Above: *This preformed plant-plug will get specimen plants off to a good start. Bury plug in the aquarium gravel.*

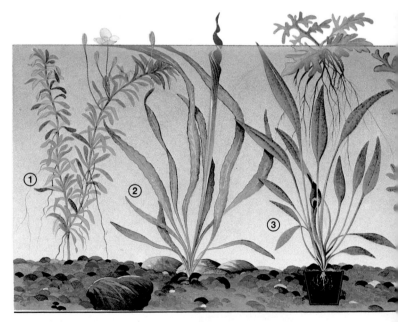

1 Egeria densa
Grows best in hard water. Absorbs nourishment through the leaves.
2 Cryptocoryne balansae
Long leaves make it ideal for a deep tank. Flowers above the surface in shallow water. Spreads by runners.

3 Cryptocoryne willisii
Variable in size. An extremely useful foreground plant shown here pot-planted, which allows it to be transplanted without disturbance. Will grow in shady locations and can be planted beneath taller plants.

Above: *A lavishly furnished and stocked aquarium combining a wide range of fishes and plants from various tropical regions. Such 'aquascaping' is one of the many pursuits fishkeepers can enjoy.*

4 Ceratopteris thalictroides
Can be grown rooted or as a floating subject with long trailing roots. A vigorous plant that thrives in warm brightly lit conditions, producing daughter plants on the surface of the leaves. Must be kept in check.

5 Cryptocoryne wendtii
Adaptable aquarium plant. Colour varies from one plant to another.
6 Vesicularia dubyana
A clinging moss with tiny leaves on long stems. Grow in good light and keep it clear of sediment and algae.

51

Planting

Planting is best done with the aquarium only three quarters filled with water (to avoid overflowing with water displaced by your hands and arms). Another advantage of this over planting the aquarium dry is that the plants take up their natural positions in the water and the effects of planting can be seen immediately.

Before planting, rinse each plant thoroughly, and inspect for snails' eggs, beetles or any other unwanted passengers. Species of plants can be laid out together in groups between layers of wet newspaper until required. Remove any dead leaves and trim back overlong roots.

Rooted species should be planted in the gravel so that the crown of the plant (the junction between roots and stem/leaves) is just above the gravel.

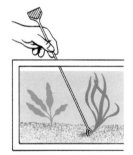

Many plants take time to assume their growing attitude and a few hours of tank-light may be needed before all the plants have finalized their positions. Clumps of cuttings may be anchored or weighted down with thin strips of lead twisted around the lower stems. Take care not to crush the stems when attaching the lead strips; bruising can be caused.

Some species of plants appear to be incompatible when grown together or expected to share the same tank. This is not surprising, for the plants come from many different localities and water conditions around the world. If you find that this is the case, a study of the plants' original habitats will enable you to select the species that should do well together.

Often biological filtration is blamed for poor plant growth, but this has not been conclusively proved. Usually a too shallow depth of gravel over the filter plate is the reason, and the simple remedy is deeper gravel.

Left: *Using a planting stick.*
Below: *Aquarium plants can be propagated from plantlets or by taking cuttings and removing the bottom leaves before planting.*
Right: *Plants soon hide essential hardware and the tank's rear wall.*

Starting up and running in

To complete the setting up, the heating, lighting, aeration and filtration equipment require final power connections to be made, but leave the moment of switching on until last. A convenient order of operations would be as follows.

Filters
External filters should be packed with layers of filter floss and activated carbon (see page 30). External filters should be filled with water by siphon action. The siphon inlet tube should be submerged until filled with water; a finger or starting stick prevents air from entering the top (short) end while the pipe is positioned over the tank edge into the filter box (keep the lower end of the siphon tube under water all this time). Remove your finger or starting stick, and water will flow into the filter box and stop automatically when the level of water rises to the same as that in the tank.

External canister-type power filters may be primed by a strong suck at their output pipe; when water flows out of this pipe, reconnect the flow pipe back to the aquarium.

Internal filters are self-priming and only need connecting to an air supply or electrical point in order to start.

Biological filters will already have their airlines connected when fitted.

Air pump
The airline from the pump should be connected to one end of the ganged control valve. Individual airlines are then connected from the control valve outlets to the airstone (if fitted) and to the air-operated filters, making sure that, if the air pump is not situated above the water level, the airline is looped above the water level for a few centimetres (see the anti-syphon loop described on page 25).

Right: *This schematic drawing shows how an air pump should be connected to a ganged control valve, which then supplies air to various pieces of equipment in the tank. The check valve and anti-siphon loop in the plastic tubing both act to prevent back-siphoning of water should the electricity supply fail to the pump.*

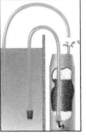

Above: *Priming filters.* Top: *Use a starting stick over the top end of the inlet tube with the bottom end still submerged.* Centre: *A finger does the same.* Bottom: *Prime power filters with water, then fix return hose.*

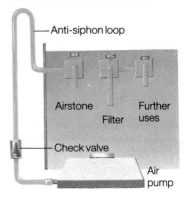

Anti-siphon loop

Airstone

Filter

Further uses

Check valve

Air pump

Thermometers

Fix the thermometer in a conveniently visible position (liquid crystal types are fitted to the glass externally).

Electrical connections

The supply wires to the air pump, electrically powered filter (if fitted), lighting and thermostat can now be connected to their respective terminals in the junction box or cable tidy. Note that the thermostat terminal connection is not switched whereas the air pump, lighting and other spare terminals can be switched. (The thermostat circuit must be live at all times, to maintain the heating circuit.) The wire from the separate heater is joined to the thermostat independently of the cable tidy; a combined heater/thermostat unit is wired directly to the cable tidy.

When all is finished within the tank, fit the cover glass and put the reflector/hood in place. Check that all electrical fittings are secure and watertight, and that tungsten lamps and/or fluorescent tube are fitted.

The supply wire to the cable tidy can now be connected to the mains supply and the power switched on. Hopefully, everything works!

Above, from left to right: A dial-type thermometer that sticks to the inside glass. A conventional type attached to the inside glass by a rubber sucker. A flat liquid crystal type stuck on the outside surface of the aquarium.

Below: A close-up of the cable tidy that acts as junction box for the electrical connections to aquarium equipment. Two switches and a neon warning light can be seen. The thermostat circuit is not switched.

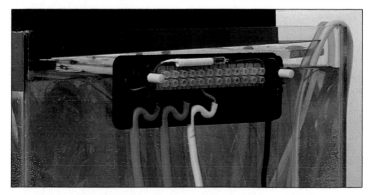

Operation

The heater circuit can be checked visually; the neon light in the cable tidy will glow as a warning that the electricity supply is connected. Neon lamps fitted to thermostats may show different information according to design. Refer to the manufacturer's instructions. If something is wrong, disconnect the power supply before investigating. Should the lights, air pump or power filter not operate, check that the switch on the cable tidy is not in the 'off' position.

If the air pump is servicing airstones and filters, or maybe an external filter and an internal biological filter, it is often the case that one will work and not the other. In this event, adjust the control valve on each air supply so that each piece of air-operated equipment functions correctly.

Above: *A neon lamp glows through the cover of the 'cable tidy' junction box to clearly indicate that the mains electricity supply is 'on'.*

Very often external power filters do not pump water immediately. This is normally due to an air lock in the system, usually at the top of the filter body. A gentle shake usually persuades the trapped air to escape up the return pipe and the water flow commences quite readily.

Running in

It will be some time before the aquarium settles down. The biological filter will take time to mature its colony of bacteria (see page 28), and the plants also need time to become established. A few hardy fishes may be introduced, to provide

Below left: A cover glass protects the light fittings from condensation and prevents plant leaves from being scorched. Keep it scrupulously clean.

waste ammonia for the bacteria to get started on, and to provide interest for you while you wait!

After a few days the plants will have taken up their normal attitudes and the water temperature will have stabilized. If no fishes have been introduced, the aquarium should be operated normally with the lighting hours observed just as if fishes were present. Of course, no food needs to be added until fishes are introduced.

Don't judge fishkeeping by your experiences in the first few weeks – you and your aquarium need to get to know each other, but the fun and real enjoyment is in the learning.

Below: The combination of tungsten and fluorescent lamps in this hood provides a balanced light output for the plants and the fishes alike.

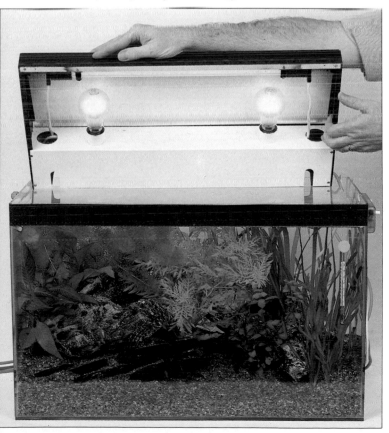

Introducing the fishes

Having carefully provided the ideal environment for the fishes, you owe it to them (and your own chances of success) to select the very best healthy stock, in correct numbers. This is not just a matter of calculating the theoretical numbers to suit the tank's fish-carrying capacity, but also involves purchasing a reasonable number (say six or more) of a species of fish that naturally lives in a shoal. Similarly, the total 'population' should be sub-divided into groups of fishes that occupy top, middle and lower levels of the aquarium water, thus ensuring that all the tank space is utilized, to give maximum room for the fish and maximum enjoyment for you as a 'viewer'.

When assessing a possible purchase, reject without hesitation any fish that:

1 cannot swim effortlessly, or maintain a steady position in the water.
2 has a very thin cross-section or a hollow belly.
3 has folded-down, split or frayed fins.
4 has obvious pimples, spots, wounds or other body damage.
5 is not eating regularly. (Ask the dealer; being *given* food regularly is not the same thing.)
6 has not been quarantined, or comes from a dubious source.
7 is of an extreme size, small or large, compared to its intended tankmates. (One may either eat, or be eaten by, the other.)
8 is very expensive, until you are sure that you can keep it successfully; it may need special conditions.

The change from shop tank to your tank is a traumatic experience for the fish, and it is therefore necessary to make this changeover as gentle a process as possible.

By the time the journey is completed there may be a difference in temperature between the water that the fish is in and the water in your aquarium. The bag or jar containing the new purchase should be floated in the aquarium until the water temperatures are equal, at which time the fish can be released. A recent school of thought prefers all new fishes to be transferred to an open jar before floating to equalize temperatures, as prolonged imprisonment in a plastic bag may cause a build-up of toxic gases. One advantage of using an open jar (or even an open plastic bag) is that increasing amounts of aquarium water may be added progressively during the floating period to acclimatize the fish to the quality, as well as the temperature, of the aquarium water. A special floating tank that allows gradual mixing of aquarium water to the fish's transit water is commercially available.

Many fishkeepers switch off the aquarium lighting when introducing new fishes, and even give the existing tenants a pinch or two of food to take their minds off the newcomers.

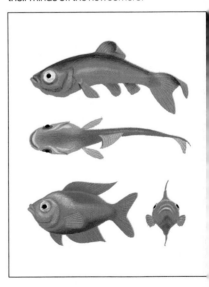

Above: *Fishes with hollow bellies and emaciated bodies as shown here are not necessarily hungry – they may be suffering from fish diseases.*

Right: *This selection of fishes would be suitable for a mixed community aquarium. They will make use of all levels in the tank and provide a striking mixture of shape, colour and swimming habit. Avoid mixing boisterous and timid fishes.*

Above: Float the bag of new fishes in the water for about twenty minutes.

Above: When the temperatures have equalized release them carefully.

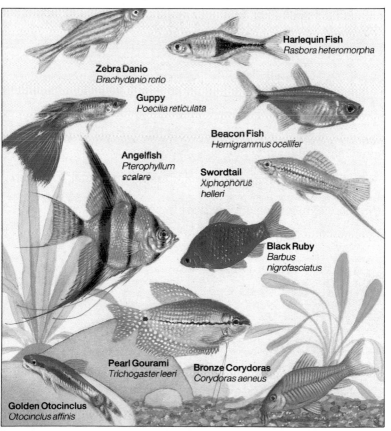

Zebra Danio
Brachydanio rerio

Harlequin Fish
Rasbora heteromorpha

Guppy
Poecilia reticulata

Beacon Fish
Hemigrammus ocellifer

Angelfish
Pterophyllum scalare

Swordtail
Xiphophorus helleri

Black Ruby
Barbus nigrofasciatus

Pearl Gourami
Trichogaster leeri

Bronze Corydoras
Corydoras aeneus

Golden Otocinclus
Otocinclus affinis

Feeding

In nature, fishes are restricted to what food is brought to them by water currents, what food falls into the river, or maybe whatever food they themselves can catch.

Much of the fish's diet consists of insects, which may fall into the water from branches of overhanging trees, or may be washed from low bushes by rising floodwaters. Water-dwelling insects, small amphibians, and crustaceans are also obvious sources of nourishment. Many fish are vegetarian and browse on water plants and algae; and some South American species are fruit-eaters. Big fishes eat smaller or ailing ones, and the aquarium world has its share of predatory, carnivorous species.

Keeping fishes in captivity, the hobbyist must provide a diet for them, and, faced with the above shopping list, it may be difficult to imagine where to begin. Distant memories of cardboard tubs of ants' eggs might come to mind, but – like the goldfish bowl – these have (or should have) become extinct and form no part of modern fishkeeping practice on diet. What, then, keeps our fishes from starving?

Manufactured foods

Just as technology has moved pogressively forward in other areas of fishkeeping, so too has research into fishes' dietary needs and the means of fulfilling them. At one time, manufactured fish foods were based largely on cereals, but it was soon realized that these were deficient in many ways. Vitamins (a list of which would not disgrace the side of any human packaged food) were tentatively added, together with lean meats and oils. Eventually, the crumbly, dried foods evolved into today's flake, granular, powdered and liquid foods; there are many different diets, of high-protein, vegetable and carnivore foods, and special formulas for young fishes hardly able to swim.

A further welcome addition came with the development of freeze-drying techniques. This meant that living waterborne creatures that normally form the major part of fishes' food could be processed, retaining the original nutritional value and only lacking (for the fish) the thrill of the hunt. Freeze-dried foods (which may also be gamma-irradiated for disinfection) include *Daphnia, Tubifex* worms, *Mysis* shrimps and other crustaceans.

Theoretically, feeding problems have been solved, with all the requirements met, and handy straight off the shelf. There are, however, one or two other factors to be taken into consideration.

Just like humans, a fish may find the same food monotonous and refuse to feed, or at least appear reluctant to do so. Another, more serious, danger with a monotonous diet is that the fish may well be denied vital ingredients over a period of time and not grow fully, even losing its resistance to disease.

The amount of food given is very important, or rather the amount of food eaten; it is essential that the fishkeeper learns to judge the amount of food required at each feeding as accurately as possible. It is far better to leave the fishes looking for more than to give them more than they need. It is not that a fish will over-eat. The problem is the surplus, uneaten food remaining in the tank, which, unless it is removed by the fishkeeper, soon decomposes and pollutes the aquarium. The second most important rule in fishkeeping (after don't overstock the aquarium) is don't overfeed.

For each fish to develop its best colours, size and a vigorous, healthy constitution, a varied diet is needed. This can be provided by using several different brands of the many excellent dried foods available, but the fish's diet is better served by the use of live foods from time to time.

Live foods

Waterborne insects, worms and crustaceans, even from cold waters, are eagerly eaten by tropical fishes. The fishkeeper who has access to a pond may be in a position to collect his own fish food, but the foods caught must be screened so that predacious insect larvae are not

Above: *A selection of dried foods.* **1** *Multiflavoured flake.* **2** *Floating pellets.* **3** *Freeze-dried Tubifex cubes.* **4** *Flour-fine food suitable for fry.* **5** *Stick-on tablet food.* **6** *Granulated high protein food.* **7** *Freeze-dried shrimp.* **8** *Vegetable flake food. Tubed liquid fry food is also available.*

introduced into the aquarium. Dangerous larvae include those of the greater diving beetle (*Dytiscus marginalis*), water boatmen (*Notonecta* sp), whirligig beetle (*Gyrinus* sp.) and dragonflies (*Aeshna, Libellula, Sympetrum*). Other unwanted pondlife are *Hydra* and leeches, together with fish parasites *Argulus, Dactylogyrus* and *Gyrodactylus* (see the section on diseases, particularly page 75).

Tubifex worms are found in harvestable numbers only in sewage-polluted waters, and their feeding to fishes may be suspect, although if kept under running water prior to use in the aquarium they may be quite safe. *Daphnia* (the water flea) and *Cyclops* are also good live foods although not all fishes take *Cyclops*

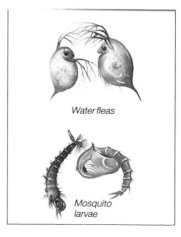

Water fleas

Mosquito larvae

Above: *Collect mosquito larvae and water fleas and use as live foods.*

(which may also chase very young fishes in the aquarium).

Nearer home, the contents of a garden rain-butt will yield good live foods such as mosquito and gnat larvae. Another excellent food is the earthworm, either small specimens, or larger ones cut into segments if you can bear to do it.

The fishkeeper can also culture live foods, which are grown in compost and fed with cereal foods, a successive culture being started as another ends its useful life. Such foods include white worms, grindal worms and micro-worms, all species of *Enchytraeus*.

A major cultured food, particularly valuable as live food for newly born fishes, is *Artemia salina*, the brine shrimp. Eggs of this saltwater crustacean may be stored dry indefinitely; when they are immersed in salt water, the hatched nauplii may be fed to the young fishes. In addition to being a live, nutritious food, brine shrimps also have the advantage over pond-caught microscopic life (*Infusoria*, rotifers, etc.) that they are entirely disease-free. Eggs are commercially available in two forms –

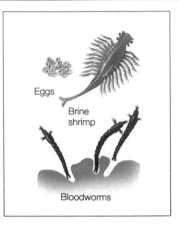

Above: *Eggs of brine shrimps can be hatched easily in warm salt water. Bloodworms are also excellent food.*

with or without shells – and a higher yield is gained from the latter.

The warning about not giving too much dried food does not apply in the case of waterborne live foods; as long as these foods remain alive no pollution will occur, and their extra oxygen demand will not be a strain on the aquarium. But live foods from

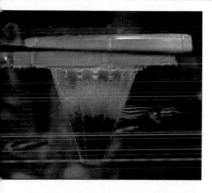

Above: *This floating worm dispenser is ideal for surface-feeding fishes.*

Above: *The carnivorous nature of the Piranha is clear from its sharp teeth.* Left: *Congo Tetras feeding on a wriggling mass of live* Tubifex *worms.*

terrestrial sources – earthworms, insects, etc. – may only survive for a short period under water and should be removed if not eaten.

Other foods

Household foods can also be considered for fishes. Ox-heart is an established favourite meat food; this and other lean raw meats can be offered. Vegetable foods such as lettuce, peas, spinach and wheatgerm are all appreciated and may be instrumental in diverting your fishes' attention away from the aquarium plants. An inventive fishkeeper may well try other foods, but the fishes will have to be introduced to each new flavour gradually. Remove uneaten food to prevent it decomposing.

Feeding advice

Make a point of watching your fish feed and see how much they consume at any one feeding time, over a period of a few minutes. Fishes often come to the surface (or the front glass of the aquarium) when anyone approaches them, but this should not be a signal to feed them. If the whole family is interested in looking after the aquarium, make sure that everyone knows when the fishes have just been fed, or fix certain feeding times each day, so that over-feeding does not occur.

At holiday times it is questionable whether to entrust the feeding to non-fishkeeping neighbours; they are prone to over-feed! Previously well-fed fish are quite capable of doing without food for two weeks, and may well have 'cleaned up' the tank by the time of your return.

Bottom dwelling fishes should not be looked upon merely as scavengers. These species, together with other nocturnal species, should be given their food after the aquarium lights have been switched off.

Brine shrimp eggs are hatched in a solution of rock salt (20grm to 1 litre/3.2oz to 1 gallon of fresh water). At a temperature of 24°C (75°F) they hatch in 24-36 hours.

When feeding newly born fishes, do not give the food until they are able to take it, otherwise tank pollution will occur.

In order that surface-swimming fishes can take food that normally sinks fast – for instance, *Tubifex* worms – plastic floating worm feeders can be used; these allow the worms to escape very slowly, and the fishes can take them at their leisure. The perforated container can be removed and the holder used as a feeding ring; this prevents food from floating all over the aquarium and accustoms the fishes to expect food at a certain place.

Finally, a fish's favourite food in the aquarium is often – fish; the young fry of live-bearing fishes are not likely to survive in a community tank, nor newly laid eggs from egg-laying species. It is not surprising, therefore, that cod's roe makes good fish food.

Maintenance

The claim was made at the beginning of this book that relatively small effort need be exerted by the fishkeeper to maintain an aquarium in good health. Having the aquarium furnished with the first fishes swimming around is only a start, but what may be seen as chores are not too arduous.

Fish watching becomes addictive, but you should watch with a purpose as well as for pleasure. At feeding time, do a spot check on the number of fishes. Any repeated absentee should be searched for; it may be a normally nocturnal species having a sleep during the hours of 'tanklight', but the cause may be more serious. A dead fish undetected will pollute the tank and, if diseased, may posthumously infect the rest of the tank's inmates.

Water temperature can be monitored with a glance at the conveniently placed thermometer, although you will soon become expert at knowing the water temperature by the touch of your hand on the front glass.

Plants may need attention, too; remove dead leaves, prune the more rampant species, and start new plants from the cuttings. Specimen plants may be given regular food tablets to promote healthy growth.

MAINTENANCE CHECK	Daily	Weekly	Monthly	Periodically
Check water temperature and number of fishes	●	●	●	●
Water condition Check pH				●
Partial change of water			●	
Filters Box filter: Clean and replace medium according to amount of use and state of aquarium				●
Undergravel filter: Rake the aquarium gravel gently				●
Plants Remove dead leaves and excess sediment on leaves; thin out floating plants		●	●	●
Prune; replant cuttings and runners as necessary		●	●	●
General Check air supply carefully; clean air pump valves and air pump filter				●
Clean cover glass				●
Remove algae from front glass of aquarium				●
Check fishes for symptoms of diseases				●

Note: If your fishes start to behave oddly, it may be worth checking over the tasks outlined above – regular aquarium maintenance can keep them healthy.

Water conditions are kept stable by regular partial water changes, 10-20% being replaced every 2-3 weeks. Tests to check pH and hardness levels are not obligatory but should be made if sudden fish losses occur for any unexplained reason. When you set up an aquarium for breeding purposes, attention to water conditions may be more vital.

Any growth of algae on the front glass should be removed, but not those on the rear and side walls of the aquarium; vegetarian fishes will do this job for you and benefit into the bargain.

The sudden switching off or on of the aquarium lights may shock some fishes, which often dash about aimlessly in the tank as a result. Short of fitting dimmer controls, the best way of avoiding this risk is to leave the room light on for a few minutes after switching the aquarium lights off. Similarly, switch the room lights on for a few minutes (unless daylight is present) before switching the tank lights on again in the morning.

Keep cover glasses scrupulously clean, and replace any defective lamps. Filter medium replacement should be a regular, unneglected commitment. When servicing external power filters, pay particular attention to the secureness of the hose connections. Filters on air pumps and in airlines should also receive regular attention. Blocked airstones should be replaced, although sometimes boiling them cleans them out again.

The behaviour of the fishes, although not quite so relevant in a maintenance scheme, should also be noted. Transfer any ailing fish at once to a hospital tank (and make sure the tank components are serviceable, too). This hospital/quarantine tank can also be on standby to act as a breeding tank if fishes show signs of courtship behaviour.

The accompanying table gives a guide to the normal maintenance schedule. Itemized operations may be omitted or re-scheduled according to your particular set-up of aquarium equipment and the type of fishes that you keep.

Useful equipment

Servicing an aquarium can almost be done with the bare hands, but there are implements available which make some routine jobs easier, quicker and a lot less messy.

Items used when setting up the aquarium will be of use also during the normal maintenance of the aquarium.

Planting sticks, despite their name, seem to be of more use *after* the tank has been planted and become established. During the original planting, it always seems easier to use one's fingers, probably because clumps, and not many individual plants, are being put into position.

Above: *The simplest way to make partial water changes is to siphon water from the floor of the aquarium using a length of tubing; detritus is removed at the same time.*

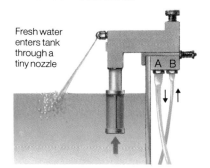

Fresh water enters tank through a tiny nozzle

Above: *An automatic water changer that works by water pressure alone. Fresh water (B) enters via a nozzle as a preset amount of old water (A) drains; the level remains constant.*

Later on, however, the thin planting stick is more easily used in a thickly planted tank, where bulkier fingers might do more damage. Some planting sticks double as algae-scrapers, having a razor blade fixture at the other end. (A razor blade is always useful – for cutting airline to length, chopping up meaty foods, trimming plant roots, etc. – and it is handy to know where one is to be found for these jobs.)

The hose that was used to fill the tank can equally be used to empty some of the water out during partial water changes. This water should be drawn from the floor of the aquarium, so that any detritus is removed at the same time. Detritus can also be removed by the use of what can only be described as an aquarium vacuum-cleaner – an air-lift device (operated from the aquarium air pump) which discharges into a cloth bag where the dirt is trapped, the water running through back into the aquarium.

Nets of various sizes will also be needed. Square-shaped nets, with cranked handles, make the capture of obstinate fishes simpler, particularly when they flee into the corner of the aquarium and refuse to budge. Often the combined use of two nets (the larger one held stationary) brings better results. Fish nets should be made of soft material, which can be silk (for small nets for very young fishes), muslin (for catching live foods), or the more usual netting material found on commercially available fish nets. A widely opened plastic bag (invisible under water) is used by many fishkeepers to capture large fishes without damaging their scales.

Magnetic algae-cleaners have the advantage of being 'self-parking' in the aquarium; their only drawback is that if they are big enough to do the job quickly, they are unsightly when parked. Be sure to keep them well away from the thermostat; they can disrupt its functioning and cause temperature fluctuations in the water. Long-handled abrasive pads also do a good job in removing algae, or a nylon (not copper) pot scourer or

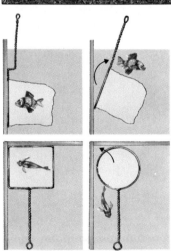

Above: *The left-hand drawings show the benefits of cranked handles and square-shaped nets over the more traditional types shown on the right.*

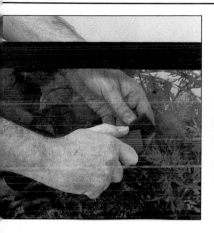

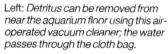

Left: *Detritus can be removed from near the aquarium floor using this air-operated vacuum cleaner; the water passes through the cloth bag.*

Above: *These self-parking abrasive pads are magnetized; as you move the outer pad the inner one clears the glass of unsightly algae growths.*

Above right: *An abrasive pad on a long handle can be useful for cleaning the aquarium glass. Leave some of the green algae on the rear and side walls as food for the fishes.*

steel wool (*not* the soap pad variety) may be used instead for this job.

Unsightly growths of algae blanketing the plants may be removed by twirling a planting stick through the growth and collecting it like candy-floss. Chemical cures are also available, which kill the algae, but it is better to attack the cause. Algae can be encouraged by too much light or, conversely, by too few aquarium plants. Over-feeding often produces excess nutrients in the water for algae to feed and multiply on. And spores of algae may be inadvertently brought into an aquarium together with wild-caught live foods.

A spiral brush fitted onto a long wire is indispensable for cleaning out long external hoses on power filters or for unclogging an undergravel filter's airlift pipe very effectively.

Breeding traps are divided floating containers in which gravid (pregnant)

female live-bearer fishes are placed to give birth; the young fishes swim into another compartment to escape from 'mum'. Unfortunately, these devices have two drawbacks: the gravid female is often disturbed by the confinement of the trap and will give birth prematurely to young fish who may not survive; and breeding traps floated in the aquarium directly beneath the aquarium lights will be in the warmest region and the high temperatures often account for many losses of fish kept in traps.

Test kits for pH, hardness and nitrites can be relied upon to give the fishkeeper accurate information as to the stability (or instability) of the aquarium water. For the beginner these kits are not absolutely necessary; for the technically curious they are mildly interesting (until the novelty wears off); but for the experienced aquarist trying to establish certain water qualities in order to breed a particularly demanding species, they are indispensable.

Automatic feeders, lighting dimmers and time clock controllers are very much *de luxe* pieces of equipment that only affluent fishkeepers have; for the average fishkeeper's absence from the aquarium during holidays (and you will not want to be away any longer than necessary), the expense of such equipment hardly merits its use, because it is much more fun to do it yourself as a *practical* fishkeeper.

Fish anatomy

Much can be learned about a fish's lifestyle by simply studying its external features and body shape.

Flowing fins indicate a slow-moving fish that inhabits slow-moving or stationary water; but torpedo-shaped bodies with large tail fins are adapted to fast-flowing streams or the open waters of large lakes.

The position of its mouth indicates from which region of the water a fish normally takes its food; an upturned mouth is ideal for surface-swimming species; a terminally situated mouth is found in mid-water feeders; and bottom-dwelling fishes have an underslung mouth, usually coupled with a flat ventral outline, though some algae-browsing fishes (which are not entirely bottom-dwelling) also have an underslung mouth.

Body covering

Most fishes are covered with scales, which provide streamlining as well as protection. Some Catfishes have rows of large, overlapping bony scutes in place of scales, and a few species have neither scales nor scutes, and are considered to be 'naked'. (Such fishes may be intolerant of medicaments.)

Fins

Generally seven in number, the fins are used for movement and stability, and in some cases as a spawning aid, during pre-spawning courtship displays, or as egg-carriers, fertilization stimuli or fry-care aids.

The caudal fin provides propulsion; in some species this fin is continuous with the dorsal and anal fins.

The dorsal fin is often extended like a sail to impress females of the species or to threaten rival males; some species have two separate dorsal fins, each with both hard and soft rays. Male fishes develop filamentous extensions to the dorsal fin with age.

An extra fatty non-erectile fin, the adipose fin, is carried by most Characins and members of the Callichthyidae family between the dorsal fin and the caudal fin.

A single fin beneath the body, the anal fin, is another stabilizing fin,

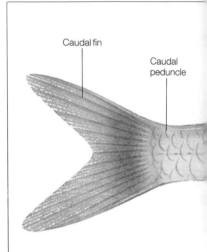

Caudal fin

Caudal peduncle

Basic fish anatomy
This cutaway drawing shows the main anatomical features of a typical fish.

which counterbalances the dorsal fin. In live-bearing fishes the anal fin is modified from the normal fan shape into a rod-like structure, the gonopodium, which is used as a reproductive organ.

Pelvic or ventral fins are paired and carried ahead of the anal fin. These fins are almost single filaments in Angelfishes and Gouramies, and the latter group can move these fins forward at will to explore their surroundings. *Corydoras* species use these fins to transport eggs to the chosen spawning site.

Pectoral fins, emerging just behind the gill covers, are used for manoeuvring, although the Hatchet fishes use them to propel themselves across the surface of the water, and some other species use them to entice the female when spawning.

Lateral line system

In addition to the same five senses that we enjoy, fishes have an extra sensory system. This is based on vibrations in the water reaching the fish's nervous system through a series of 'portholes' along its flanks – the so called lateral line system.

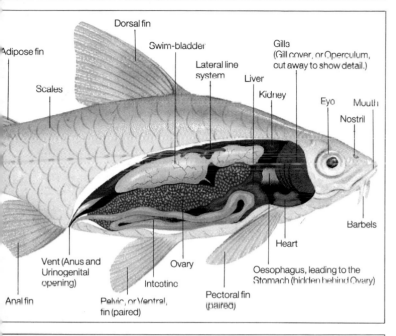

Dorsal fin

Swim-bladder

Adipose fin

Lateral line system

Gills (Gill cover, or Operculum, cut away to show detail.)

Scales

Liver

Kidney

Eye

Mouth

Nostril

Barbels

Heart

Vent (Anus and Urinogenital opening)

Ovary

Oesophagus, leading to the Stomach (hidden behind Ovary)

Intestine

Anal fin

Pectoral fin (paired)

Pelvic, or Ventral, fin (paired)

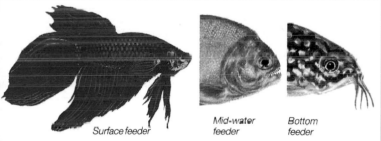

Surface feeder

Mid-water feeder

Bottom feeder

Above: *Fishes with mouths adapted for different feeding methods.*

In dark murky waters some fishes navigate or locate their prey by electro-magnetism, but the Blind Cave Fish relies on its lateral line system to find its way about.

Swim-bladder
When stationary, fishes maintain their position in the water by means of a hydrostatic buoyancy organ known as the swim-bladder.

Colour
Colour is used by fishes to identify species and sex. It also serves as camouflage and as a sexual stimulus. It is produced in two ways: reflection, and pigmentation. Layers of *guanin* (a waste product from the kidneys, but not excreted from the body) beneath the scales reflect the light, giving fishes their familiar iridescent colours. Other colours are produced by cells called chromatophores, and these cells may be contracted or expanded at will. A frightened, angry or otherwise excited fish can either fade or intensify its colours. Several species change their colours during the hours of darkness, and can be seen in different patterns early each morning before reverting to normal daylight colouring again.

Diseases

Fishes will succumb to disease from time to time, but most diseases are easily recognized and successfully treated. However, the fishkeeper can do much, by following a few simple guidelines, to ensure that his fishes do not contract disease. The best deterrents to poor fish health are careful choice of original stock, quarantine and good aquarium hygiene at all times.

The selection of healthy stock is described elsewhere (page 58), but even apparently healthy additions to the aquarium should be quarantined. Isolate new stock in a spare tank for 2-3 weeks, during which time any latent disease should manifest itself. If any disease does occur, the quarantine tank can immediately be converted into a hospital tank.

Aquarium plants can also introduce unwanted guests into the aquarium and new plants should be thoroughly rinsed before use; a bath in a weak solution of potassium permanganate will destroy any minute aquatic life on plant leaves.

External factors should also be considered. Fumes from paint, cigarette smoke, air sprays and furniture polish can all be carried into the aquarium through the air pump. Avoid using materials giving off strong fumes or vapours near to the aquarium, and do not put hands recently washed with strong soap (or dirty hands not washed at all!) into the aquarium water.

Aquarium nets can spread diseases from tank to tank, so each tank should be allocated its own net, which must be disinfected after each use. Moving fishes from tank to tank if there is any suspicion of disease is asking for trouble.

Wherever possible, avoid any metal/water contact. The metal spring clip holding on an external thermostat can be covered with a length of airline to prevent contact with the water.

Be sure to maintain correct water temperatures, clean filters regularly and make partial water changes a habit. These actions, together with a full varied diet, will ensure that your fishes remain at the peak of fitness.

Treatments

Treatments for disease range from individual baths to medication of the whole tank. In some cases, treatment can be administered internally by soaking the fish's food in the medication before feeding, but gauging the amount taken is somewhat difficult! Occasionally, a fish may be treated out of water, when dealing with a wound or a parasitic infection large enough to be treated in this way.

Filters used in any tank that is to be treated should not contain carbon, as it will adsorb the medication; and extra aeration should be used, because medicaments often reduce the level of oxygen in the water. Aquarium plants are sometimes

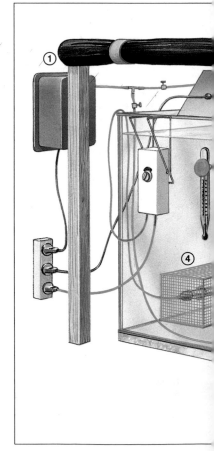

adversely affected, and fine-leaved species suffer most.

At the end of any treatment the fishes should be acclimatized gradually to normal water conditions by the partial replacement of medicated water with fresh clean water over a period of days.

Below: *A fish carrying a parasitic anchor worm (Lernaea) on its back.*

The hospital aquarium (Below)
1 *The blinds can be lowered to prevent light reaching the aquarium and affecting the medication. The hood lights would be turned off.*
2 *A simple internal box filter is used containing no activated carbon that would adsorb medications.*
3 *A few flowerpots and plastic plants give the fishes a feeling of security. Plastic plants are used because live ones could be damaged by some medications being given.*
4 *The heater is controlled by an easily adjusted external thermostat and caged in to prevent damage to fishes sheltering nearby.*
5 *The airstone provides a bubble stream to circulate warmth and keep the oxygen level high in the tank.*

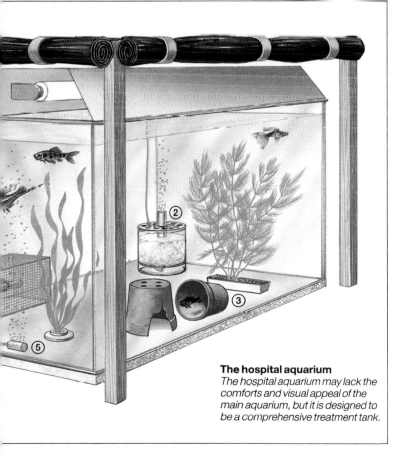

The hospital aquarium
The hospital aquarium may lack the comforts and visual appeal of the main aquarium, but it is designed to be a comprehensive treatment tank.

71

Fish diseases
Illustrated here are some of the more common ailments that befall fishes in the aquarium. Some are due to parasites introduced into the aquarium with live foods or plants from other waters; others are bacterial infections brought about by poor aquarium hygiene and lack of maintenance.

Tailrot/Finrot
These very obvious symptoms appear on fishes of poor health. Low temperatures, physical damage, and unhygienic conditions in the aquarium all encourage the harmful bacterial action.

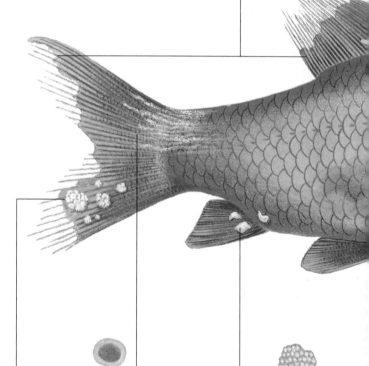

Lymphocystis
This conditions causes cauliflower-like growths to appear on the fins and the skin. At the same time the fish loses weight. Individual cell growth is rapid. This condition is rarely found among freshwater fishes.

Fungus
Fungus *(Saprolegnia)* attacks fishes already weakened by physical damage, parasites, or poor conditions. Also liable to affect fishes if they are transferred to widely differing aquarium waters.

Pox
White spots join to form large patches. Affected fishes become emaciated and are often left twisted. Faulty diet and lack of vitamins are likely causes. May heal itself under good aquarium conditions.

White spot
Tiny white spots cover the fins and body. A very common parasitic ailment that some aquarists believe lies dormant in every aquarium ready to afflict weak fishes.

Velvet disease
Infected fishes have a dusty appearance. Caused by a parasite *Oodinium*, which goes into an encystment stage. Will respond well to widely available proprietary cures.

Skin flukes
The *Gyrodactylus* parasites burrow into the fish's skin and stay near the surface. Affected fishes lose colour and become feeble. Responds well to treatments.

Eye infections
Cloudy eyes (below) are often due to eye fungus or to worm cataract, *Proalaria*. Protruding eyes (main illustration) usually suggest that other diseases are present as well.

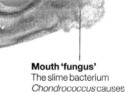

Mouth 'fungus'
The slime bacterium *Chondrococcus* causes this. It is unrelated to body fungus.

Slimy skin
Fishes afflicted with this condition develop a thin grey film over the body. The parasites *Cyclochaeta* and *Costia* (shown at above left, right) cause the fish to produce excessive amounts of slime.

Dropsy
The scales protrude noticeably due to accumulated liquid in the body. The fluid from infected fish may infect others. To prevent this happening remove any sick fishes from the aquarium promptly.

Gill flukes
The flatworm *Dactylogyrus* attaches itself to the delicate gill membranes and causes an extremely obvious inflammation. Affected fishes develop an increased respiration rate and gaping gills.

White spot disease

(Ichthyophthiriasis) This is the most common parasitic ailment and probably the easiest to diagnose. The fish's body is covered with tiny white spots, which extend to cover the fins. The disease is of a cyclic nature: the parasite leaves the fish's body to form cysts on the aquarium floor and upon hatching the parasite is then free-swimming, seeking a new host. It can be attacked by treatment at this stage. As the disease is likely to affect all the fishes in an aquarium, the whole tank should be treated. Proprietary cures are readily available, simple to administer, and extremely effective.

Velvet This disease is also fairly easy to diagnose. The fish appears to be covered by a layer of fine golden dust, giving it a velvety look. The parasite responsible, *Oodinium limneticum*, undergoes an encystment stage similar to that of the white spot disease parasite. *O. pillularis* is reponsible for another 'velvet' disease, where the colour is more of a brown colour. Established long-term bath cures included methylene blue and acriflavine, but these have been largely superseded by broad-spectrum proprietary remedies.

Fungus *(Saprolegnia)* In this disease outbreaks of cotton-wool-like tufts appear on the fish's body, or it may be covered completely with a fine layer of cobwebby or dusty fungus. An outdated treatment was to immerse the suffering fish in a salt bath. Proprietary treatments, such as Liquitox and Furanace, are much more effective.

Often confused with body fungus is mouth fungus, which is caused by a slime bacterium, and may not be cured effectively by all treatments suggested for body fungus. Phenoxethol has been successful. Antibiotics can be used but these must be obtained from a qualified veterinarian.

'Shimmying' The symptoms are aptly described; the fish makes rapid undulating movements without any

Above: *The infection cycle for white spot disease.* **1** *The afflicted fish shows the symptoms and the parasites leave the body.* **2** *Cysts form on the tank floor.* **3** *The cysts produce free-swimming parasites.*

forward movement occurring. One cause of this ailment is a drop in water temperature, so that the fish becomes chilled. The obvious remedy is to check the aquarium's heating system for any malfunction and to raise the temperature to the correct level. One species in particular seems prone to 'shimmying' – the very popular Black Molly (*Poecilia* hybrid).

Dropsy Occasionally a fish's body becomes bloated to such a degree that the scales protrude outwards. This is due to the body cavities filling with liquid. There is some confusion as to what causes this. It is difficult to cure and can be contagious, so isolate the affected fish until it recovers or has to be destroyed.

Finrot Degeneration of the tissue between individual rays of the fins is caused by bacterial infection, often encouraged by poor water conditions. The fins may have been damaged by bad handling techniques, or by a bullying fish. This allows the bacterial infection to gain a hold on the injured fins. A general

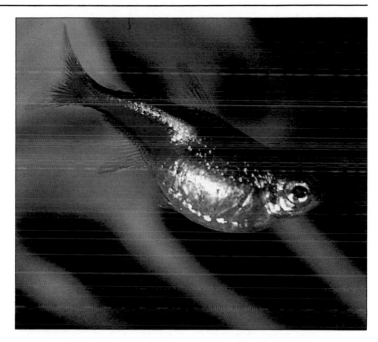

clean-up of the aquarium water is required, together with better aquarium management in the future. Proprietary cures will assist rapid recovery to full fin health, but these medicines cannot overcome neglect.

Gill flukes Fishes are sometimes seen scratching themselves on rocks or plants, accompanied by an increased respiration rate with the gills gaping and obviously inflamed. Such fishes are infected with *Dactylogyrus* or *Gyrodactylus* parasites, which burrow into the skin or collect on the delicate membranes. The parasites may be removed by bathing the fish in well-aerated solutions of proprietary treatments specially formulated for parasitic control, such as Paratox and Clout.

The parasites cannot survive without a fish host, so if the aquarium is left uninhabited for a few days while the fishes are being treated with proprietary medicaments, the parasites will be eliminated.

It is often easy to jump to the wrong conclusion. Fishes panting at the surface may not be afflicted by parasites at all, but gasping for

Above: *A Neon Tetra* (Paracheirodon innesi) *with abdominal dropsy, where fluid has accumulated in the body.*

oxygen because of an excess of carbon dioxide in the water. Immediate relief can be provided by extra aeration, but better aquarium management is the real answer.

Serious diseases
More serious ailments result from internal causes such as tuberculosis, threadworms and tapeworms, which are unseen by the fishkeeper. Usually when the symptoms become apparent it is too late to effect a cure. Diagnosis of these conditions can be done only by examination of the organs of the diseased fish (which in practical terms means a post-mortem) and this aspect of disease is beyond the capability of the beginning aquarist.

There are several diagnostic services available, but as these will only reveal the cause of death (from examination of the corpse), this course of action, which can be rather expensive, may be regarded as a little too retrospective in most cases.

Breeding

A large proportion of fishes kept in captivity will breed, often despite the conditions under which they are kept. These spontaneous breedings may go unnoticed by the aquarist, who may assume that, because the fish population's total number has not increased, nothing has been happening in the aquarium.

In the activity of the community tank, a pair of fishes may have difficulty in finding a territory in which to raise a family. Eggs from a spawning of egg-scattering fish will be accepted as a meal by the other occupants of the tank; and newly born live-bearer fry will also be harassed by more adult fishes. In order to survive, young fishes need protection, and that means a separate breeding tank with the fishkeeper playing a major role to ensure successful breeding.

There are three phases in fish breeding: pre-spawning activity, the actual spawning, and the raising of the young fry to maturity. It helps if the fishkeeper has some advance knowledge about the probable sequence of events so that appropriate arrangements can be made. The fishkeeper should know what method of spawning any of his fishes will use, how to prepare a suitable aquarium for them, and how to look after the young fry.

Methods of spawning
The majority of aquarium fishes are egg-layers, and external fertilization of the eggs occurs in several different ways. Parental care of the young is sometimes practised.

A small number of fishes are live-bearers; internal fertilization and development of the eggs occur within the female fish's body. The young fishes are born as free-swimming miniatures of their parents.

Egg-laying species
Fishes in this group fall into five categories; egg-scattering, egg-burying or egg-depositing fishes, nest-builders and mouth-brooders. Their parental care ranges from the non-existent to utter devotion.

Egg-scattering species normally inhabit flowing waters where their fertilized eggs are swept away upon release. In an aquarium the lack of water movement makes the eggs easy prey for the spawning adult

Egg-scatterers
The Zebra Danios (Brachydanio rerio) scatter their eggs and will eat them before they fall out of reach.

Egg-buriers
The egg-burying Argentine Pearlfish (Cynolebias bellotti) needs a deep layer of peat on the aquarium floor.

fishes, who will not hesitate to eat their own eggs. To overcome this otherwise abrupt halt in the breeding process the fishkeeper needs a breeding aquarium that will prevent the fishes from reaching their own eggs. Details of such designs can be found on page 80.

Egg-burying species are native to waters that totally dry out each year; only by laying their eggs in the mud (where they await the rainy season before hatching) can the species guarantee further continuance. The aquarist has to provide a layer of peat on the floor of the aquarium to allow these fishes to spawn in their accustomed manner.

Egg-depositing fishes may be secretive spawners or open water spawners. The former choose small caves (or flowerpots, in an aquarium) in which to deposit their eggs; the latter are quite happy with flat rocks, broad-leaved plants or hollows dug out of the gravel. In all cases, the site is pre-cleaned and defended; the eggs are guarded, cleaned and often moved to other pre-cleaned sites before hatching occurs. When free-

swimming, the fry are guarded and escorted around by their parents, who drive off any other fishes that venture too near.

Nest-builders need no help from the fishkeeper, building their nests from bubbles of saliva blown by the male fish, and often incorporating fragments of water plants in the nest construction. The aquarium should be densely planted to offer some shelter to the female, who may be harassed severely by the male fish after spawning is completed.

Mouth-brooding species have a two-stage spawning act. The eggs are laid by the female, usually in a depression in the gravel, and then fertilized by the male. The eggs are then picked up by the female, who incubates them in her buccal cavity, during which time she takes no food.

Live-bearing fishes
The popular species within this group will produce young at approximately monthly intervals. A single mating can produce successive broods, as the female can store the male fish's spermatozoa within her body. Other

Egg-depositors
'Kribs' (Pelvicachromis pulcher) *are secretive spawners and prefer the privacy of a flowerpot or rocky cave.*

Bubble-nest builders
Siamese Fighters (Betta splendens) *lay their eggs in a mass of bubbles they produce at the water surface.*

Left: *Spraying Characins* (Copella arnoldi) *spawning on the underside of a leaf above the water's surface. The male and female swim vertically to the surface, flick their tails and leap as much as 6cm(2.4in) up to a leaf. The female lays between five and eight eggs and these are immediately fertilized by the male. This procedure is repeated many times until hundreds of eggs have been eventually laid on the overhanging leaf.*

Left: *The female live-bearer's anal fin is fan-shaped; the male's is modified (fully or partly, depending on genus) into a functional reproductive organ.*
Right: *Jewel Cichlids* (Hemichromis bimaculatus) *spawning on a piece of wood. Both parents guard the eggs and tend the young.*

Mouth-brooders
The female Egyptian Mouth-brooder (Pseudocrenilabrus multicolor) *incubates the eggs in her mouth, taking no food until they hatch.*

species of live-bearers do not share this facility and require mating to occur for each brood. A thickly planted aquarium is recommended as a nursery tank for the pregnant female and her subsequent brood (see breeding traps, page 81).

Preparation for spawning
Whichever species you hope to breed you must start by selecting a true pair – a male and a female fish. Fortunately, this is straightforward in the live-bearing fishes, because the male fish has the anal fin modified into the reproductive organ known as the *gonopodium*. The female's anal fin is the normal fan-shape. The sex of egg-laying species can be determined by educated guesswork or by observation of the fishes' behaviour; usually, the male fish is slimmer and more colourful, and often has more elongated fins. Alternatively, particularly with egg-depositing species, the behaviour of

the fishes may be more informative; if two fish constantly keep together, and drive away other fishes from their locality, it is likely that they are a true pair, but finding out which sex is which is still a problem.

Fishes chosen for breeding must be healthy and full of vigour. The two sexes should be separated, and fed especially well on live and high-quality dried foods. This separation need not be practised with fish that have spontaneously paired off – all they need is good food and a little privacy.

If tank space is limited, a tank can be subdivided into two separate compartments to accommodate the prospective parents. It is usual to

introduce the conditioned female into the breeding tank first, before the male; in this way he has to court her in her own territory. Otherwise, if the reverse procedure is followed, she may be liable to attack.

Slightly different factors arise with live-bearing species, who will mate with complete abandon regardless of colour variety within the same species. Very careful isolation of sexes and colour varieties is required to prevent the purity of the strain from becoming unstable. The gravid (pregnant) female should be moved to the densely planted nursery tank well before her estimated delivery time to prevent premature births.

1

These illustrations show techniques fishkeepers can use to aid the breeding process in a wide range of fishes.
1 Separating the male and female for two or three weeks and feeding them with high quality and live foods ensures that both fishes are in peak condition for spawning and are keen to do so. They can be reunited simply by removing the clear partition between them.
2 A layer or two of marbles on the tank floor provides a fish-proof egg trap to prevent the adult fishes – in this case Tiger Barbs (Barbus tetrazona) – from eating the eggs. The shallow water level reduces the time that the falling eggs are at risk. Remove the eggs once spawning is over.
3 Another egg-saving device is a net draped in the water, through which the eggs fall to safety. Zebra Danios, shown here, may be spawned as a shoal.
4 Tetras lay adhesive eggs that may be trapped in a dense clump of plants where the female has been vigorously driven by the male fish to spawn.
5 Some Killifishes bury their eggs. There should be a deep layer of peat to accommodate such species as Cynolebias, shown here. After spawning, the peat (complete with the fertilized eggs) can be removed and stored almost dry for a few months. The hatching process is activated by immersing the peat in the aquarium water.

2

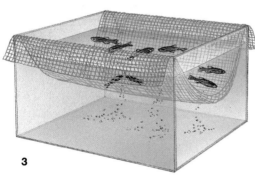

3

4

6 *Other Killifishes (such as the* Aphyosemion *shown here) lay their eggs on artificial mops, from which they can be collected and hatched in separate shallow dishes.*

7 *Depending on the species, Cichlids will require rocks, pieces of slate, flowerpots or broad-leaved plants as spawning sites. If the fishes lay their eggs in rocky caves or in flowerpots the hobbyist may not be aware that spawning has taken place until the parents bring their free-swimming youngsters out into the open.*

8 *Live-bearers can give birth in breeding traps. The fry escape to safety and should be raised in a separate, heavily planted nursery tank.*

9 Top: *A floating breeding trap that can be floated in the main aquarium. After giving birth, the female should be rested for a few days before being released into the main tank.* Bottom: *Two pieces of glass quickly convert a spare tank into a live-bearer's nursery.*

5

6

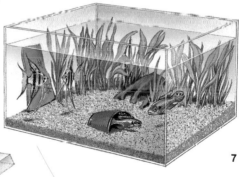

7

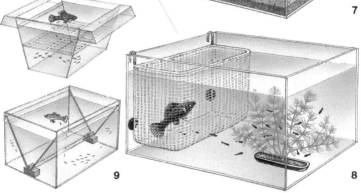

9

8

Spawning and after

Spawnings should be supervised, not just to see what occurs but also to protect the eggs or the female fish. Many male fishes will continue to harass the female after spawning; other males may not even accept the female as a partner at the outset, and she must be rescued from his violent attacks. The adult egg-scattering fishes should both be removed from the breeding tank after spawning is completed.

The eggs of the egg-burying species should be collected – still in the substrate or peat layer – and stored until re-immersing in water commences the hatching process.

Eggs deposited in plants or artificial spawning mops should be picked from the spawning medium and hatched in shallow water. Egg-depositors should be given the chance to rear their own young, but if they prove to be irresponsible parents the eggs can be hatched by using an airstone to substitute for the parent fishes' fin-fanning actions after the adults have been removed.

The male fishes of nest-building species take over the guarding of the nest and fry; the female should be removed for her own safety.

The female live-bearer should have a few days' rest after giving birth, before being returned to the community tank, to avoid undue early harassment by male fishes.

Care of the young fishes

Until the young fish swims freely it obtains nourishment from its attached yolk-sac, and it will not need food from the fishkeeper until that time. First foods can be proprietary liquid or powdered foods, formulated for either egg-layer or live-bearer young. Green water, micro-worms and grindal worms can be offered, but the best food is brine shrimp (see Feeding, page 62). As the fishes grow, the size and amount of the food should be increased. Aeration in the rearing tank should be used to keep the food moving; a simple sponge filter (as shown on page 31) is safest and will not trap fry. Weak, malformed young fish should be removed.

Above: *Rosy Barbs spawning. The reddish male nudges the female until they are side by side, when the eggs are released and then fertilized.*

Final note: Keep a written record of breeding attempts, successful or not (particularly with different species). You want to be able to remember what you did, when you get it right.

Above: *The male Paradisefish (Macropodus opercularis) inspects the bubble-nest as the female turns away after the spawning embrace.*

Below: *A breeding pair of 'Kribs' (Pelvicachromis pulcher) proudly guard their free swimming fry. Spawning takes place in rocky caves.*

83

Popular Aquarium Fishes

Although there are many thousands of species of fishes (the Federation of British Aquatic Societies lists over 650 genera alone), not all are eminently suitable for a first aquarium. Some are too large, some too small to be trusted together; some require conditions that will not suit others; some may be unobtainable in your area, or simply out of your financial grasp. Within these final pages you will find a selection of fishes that will get on together; obviously there is not room to include both pictures and text to any great extent, and at this stage a pictorial guide is more exciting and informative to the beginning fishkeeper than maybe repetitive text.

The fishes illustrated are fairly representative of their family groups and may be regarded as aquarium favourites that have become established over the years.

In addition to the species found in these pages, there are many more species suitable for the aquarium; some may be very striking in colour or have more flowing fins. Others will have characteristics all of their own, particularly at breeding time, and some fishes present such a challenge that you just have to try them!

With common sense, any selection of fishes from the those illustrated here should be amiable tank-mates; but, just as with humans, there's none so queer as fish.

A final point to remember is that you are not alone in keeping fish. There are monthly periodicals for fishkeepers, and local aquarist societies and most equipment and food manufacturers operate advisory services. Find a reputable aquarium store, follow a few simple guidelines, and there is no telling how expert you will become in practically no time at all. Unless otherwise stated, the fishes shown in the following pages are males. Where two fishes are shown together the sexes (where known) are clearly indicated.

Right: *Despite its size, the Keyhole Cichlid* (Aequidens maronii) *lives peaceably with smaller fishes.*

Above: **Barbus nigrofasciatus**
A female swollen with eggs.
Right: **Barbus conchonius**
An attractive and undemanding Barb that is ideal for beginners.
Centre right: **Barbus gelius**
A popular Barb for small tanks.
Bottom right: **Barbus oligolepis**
A hardy Barb best kept in a shoal.
Below: **Barbus cumingi**
An active Barb that swims in the middle and lower water levels.

Above left:
Brachydanio albolineatus
A constantly active fish with a delicate blue sheen to the body.
Left: **Brachydanio rerio**
Another active fish which is often recommended as a species for beginners to try to breed.

Above: **Danio devario**
Female above; male below. Danios are expert jumpers so a close-fitting cover glass is essential.
Below:
Epalzeorhynchus kallopterus
This hardy fish browses on algae and any flatworms on the aquarium glass.

Above: **Rasbora vaterifloris**
A very beautiful fish that prefers subdued light in the aquarium.
Below: **Labeo bicolor**
A striking coloured species with the equally colourful common name of 'Red-tailed Black Shark'.

Right: **Rasbora heteromorpha**
These two males can be recognized by the clearly defined lower point of the triangular marking. This long-established, popular species breeds on the undersides of leaves. A similar species is Rasbora hengeli.

Above: **Aphyocharax anisitsi**
*Formerly A. rubropinnis, this lovely
shoaling fish is easy to breed but
precautions must be taken to prevent
the parents eating the eggs.*

Below: **Cheirodon axelrodi**
*Female top; male below. An
extremely attractive shoaling species
with bright red colouration that
extends the whole length of the body.*

Above: **Gymnocorymbus ternetzi**
The jet black colouration of this peaceful, easy-to-breed fish fades gradually to grey as it ages.

Below:
Hemigrammus ocellifer ocellifer
An ideal community fish with a distinctive red spot near the tail.

Above: **Micralestes interruptus**
*Two males show off their splendid fins
and colour. Females are drabber.*
Below:
Moenkhausia sanctaefilomenae
Ideally kept in a large shoal.

Above right: **Thayeria boehlkei**
*The dark stripe accentuates this fish's
oblique swimming position.*
Below right: **Carnegiella strigata**
*A surface swimmer that excels at
jumping; keep the tank covered!*

Above: **Nannostomus beckfordi**
*Variable in colour, this lovely species
looks best when kept in a shoal.*

Below: **Nannostomus espei**
*A female of this slender peaceful
species, with a more rounded body.*

Above: **Chilodus punctatus**
This head-down pose is typical of the species and helps to hide the fishes among aquatic plants.

Below: **Nannostomus trifasciatus**
In common with its relatives, this fish's colouration changes at night from three stripes to broad bars.

Above left: Aequidens maronii
This is a male, with typically elongated
and pointed dorsal and anal fins. A
peaceful Cichlid that is suitable for a
community tank, where it will breed
quite happily. Ideal for beginners.

Top: Apistogramma agassizi
A dwarf Cichlid, easily recognizable
by its spade-shaped caudal fin with
white inner borders. This is a male; the
females are less colourful and often
indistinguishable from females of
related species. The fishes will spawn
readily in upturned flowerpots.

Above: Etroplus maculatus
One of the few Cichlids from Asia, this
species lays brightly coloured eggs.
The addition of some sea salt to the
aquarium water will benefit these
estuarine fishes.

Left: Cichlasoma meeki
The vivid red colour of this male is
enough to deter any would-be
predator as he guards a large shoal of
newly swimming fry. Despite his
belligerent appearance, this Cichlid is
a peaceful, easy-to-keep fish.

Right: **Nannacara anomala**
*A small Cichlid that will defend its
territory and its young quite
ferociously. The female often
changes her colour pattern, both to
deter intruders and to help her young
to recognize her. She chases the
male away when spawning is over.
Otherwise a peaceful species.*
Below right: **Pterophyllum scalare**
*The favourite Angelfish has been
developed by skilful breeding into
many attractive colour varieties. This
is the popular marbled strain.*
Below: **Pelvicachromis pulcher**
*Cichlids are usually excellent parents,
a feature welcomed by aquarists. This
male is taking his turn at guarding the
offspring. Members of the
Pelvicachromis genus are secretive
spawners, often surprising the
fishkeeper with an unexpected
brood. Be sure to provide rocks and
some dense vegetation for shelter.*

Above: **Betta splendens**
This male Siamese Fighting Fish is one of many colour forms available. Keep males apart; they will fight.
Below: **Macropodus opercularis**
This very colourful fish – aptly known as the Paradisefish – spawns in a bubble-nest at the surface.

Above right: **Colisa chuna**
These spawning Honey Gouramies will thrive in a peaceful aquarium.
Right: **Colisa lalia**
An extremely popular dwarf species.
Below right: **Trichogaster leeri**
The male shows the red breast and belly that develop during spawning.

Above: **Aplocheilus dayi**
The male (top) has a much more iridescent body than the female below it. This surface swimmer will jump out of the tank if given the chance. Keep with larger fishes.
Above right: **Oryzias melastigma**
This photograph shows the female (below the male) just after spawning, with the eggs still attached.
Right: **Aplocheilus panchax**
An established aquarium favourite since 1899, with a beautiful red-dotted blue colouration.
Below: **Jordanella floridae**
This hardy fish has interesting breeding habits that resemble those of the brood-protecting Cichlids.

Above: **Synodontis nigriventris**
The mottled pattern of the upturned belly probably helps this Catfish to remain undetected by predatory birds. A peaceful species that is generally active during the night.
Top right: **Corydoras melanistius**
This small, well-camouflaged Catfish with short barbels swims near the bottom of the aquarium scavenging for scraps of food. Keep in a shoal.
Centre right: **Corydoras paleatus**
This is the easiest to breed of all the Corydoras Catfishes. It is ideal for a beginner, being hardy, undemanding and long-lived in the aquarium.
Right: **Pimelodella gracilis**
This is a useful fish to have in a community tank as it spends much of its time scavenging for waste food. Keep in a subdued light.

Left: **Botia sidthimunki**
*Unlike most other species of Botia,
this Loach swims above the bottom –
mostly in the middle water layers. It is
active by day and night.*

Above: **Botia macracantha**
*The striking Clown Loach is a popular
choice for community tanks.*
Below: **Botia horae**
A hardy Loach active during the night.

Above: **Xiphophorus maculatus**
*This is an excellent live-bearer for a
beginner, even though it may be
difficult for an aquarist to discover
which of the many different varieties
he is actually keeping!*
Right: **Xiphophorus helleri**
*Only the male (bottom) has the
swordlike extension to the caudal fin.
Note also the difference in shape
between the male and female anal fin.
A very popular fish the world over.*

Left: Poecilia reticulata
This is a prolific and immensely popular fish. The females may produce young every four weeks.

Above: **Poecilia hybrid**
Always popular, the velvet black colour of the Black Molly makes a striking contrast in the aquarium.

Above: **Nematocentris nigrans**
Formerly Melanotaenia nigrans, *this
active species is recognizable by its
two separate dorsal fins.*

Below: **Badis badis**
*This peaceful fish changes its colours
in keeping with its surroundings.
Suitable for a community aquarium.*

Above: Monodactylus argenteus
*A shoaling fish that appreciates some
sea salt in the water to simulate its
estuarine habitat in the wild.*

Below: Telmatherina ladigesi
*The male (bottom) typically has long
extensions to its fins. A peaceful,
brackish water species from Celebes.*

Index to Plants and Fishes

Page numbers in *italics* refer to captions to illustrations.
Text entries are shown in normal type.

115

Picture Credits

Artists
Copyright of the artwork illustrations on the pages following the artists' names is the property of Salamander Books Ltd.

Colin Newman (Linden Artists): 46-7(B), 48-9(B), 50-1, 52, 61, 62, 74

David Nockels: 58-9, 68-9, 72-3, 76-7, 78

Tudor Art Studios: 24, 25(L), 39(B), 54, 65, 66(B), 80-1

Brian Watson (Linden Artists): 12-13, 15(BR), 16-7, 19, 20(B), 21(B), 23, 26, 27, 28-9, 41, 70-1

Photographs
The publishers wish to thank the following photographers and agencies who have supplied photographs for this book. The photographs have been credited by page number and position on the page: (B) Bottom, (T) Top, (C) Centre, (BL) Bottom left etc.

Heather Angel/Biofotos: 34-5, 41 (Murray Watson), 87(B), 106-7(B), 110-111(B)

Bruce Coleman Ltd: 38-9 (Peter Davey), 87(T, Jane Burton), 89(T, Hans Reinhard)

Eric Crichton © Salamander Books Ltd: 10-11, 20(C), 21(T,C), 22-3, 25, 29(BR), 30-31, 32, 33, 36, 37, 44-5, 53, 55, 56-7, 59, 61(T), 63(T), 66-7(T)

Michael Dyers: 18

Jan-Eric Larsson: 42(B), 83(T), 88(B), 93(T), 100-101(T), 103(C), 108-9(T), 111(T)

Dick Mills: 40

Arend van den Nieuwenhuizen: Endpapers, half-title page, title page, copyright page, 42(TR), 49(T), 51, 78(T), 79, 82, 83(B), 84-5, 86, 87(C), 88(T), 89(B), 90-1, 92, 93(B), 94, 95, 96, 97, 98-9(B), 99(C), 100(B), 101(B), 102(T), 103(T,B), 104, 105, 106(T), 107(T,C), 109(B), 110(T,C), 112(B), 113(B), 114

Barry Pengilley: 43, 75, 98(T), 112(T), 113(T)

Mike Sandford: 62

W. A. Tomey: 14, 15(BL), 47(T), 63(B), 71(T), 99(T), 102(B)

Editorial assistance
Copy-editing by Maureen Cartwright.

Acknowledgments
The publishers would like to thank the following companies for their assistance in preparing this book: Interpet Ltd., Medcalf Brothers Ltd. (Hy-Flo Products), UNO Products (C. Ellson Ltd.)

PRINTED IN BELGIUM BY
proost
INTERNATIONAL BOOK PRODUCTION

Rasbora heteromorpha (*Harlequin Fish*)